THE
POWER OF
PROPERTY

Karina Barrymore

Bruce Brammall

THE
POWER OF
PROPERTY

SECURING YOUR FUTURE
THROUGH REAL ESTATE

Karina Barrymore & Bruce Brammall

Wrightbooks

First published 2006 by Wrightbooks
an imprint of John Wiley & Sons Australia, Ltd
42 McDougall Street, Milton, Qld 4064

Offices also in Sydney and Melbourne

Typeset in ITC Giovanni 10.5/14pt

National Library of Australia Cataloguing-in-Publication data:

Barrymore, Karina.

The power of property: securing your future through real
estate.

Includes index.

ISBN 0 7314 0483 1.

1. Real estate investment. I. Brammall, Bruce. II. Title.

332.63243

Cover design by Brad Maxwell

Printed in Australia by Griffin Press

10 9 8 7 6 5 4 3 2 1

Disclaimer

Contents

Disclaimers

All taxation advice given in this book is general in nature. It is
recommended that all aspiring or existing property
investors seek advice from their accountant
or a registered tax professional.

Personal income tax rates used are those set down in the 2006
federal budget for the 2006–07 financial year.

About the authors

Karina Barrymore has been a finance and property writer and analyst for 25 years. She has worked in the United Kingdom, New Zealand and Australia as well as having personal experience buying, selling, advising, building and renovating property — her 'first love'.

Her journalism career spans three decades and in that time she has covered property, personal finance, politics, superannuation and the sharemarket. She is currently personal finance editor at Australia's largest circulation daily newspaper, the *Herald Sun*. Prior to that, she spent 12 years as senior property writer for *The Australian Financial Review*, reporting and analysing the various property markets, cycles and sectors across Australia and overseas. She has also written for many magazines and corporate publications, and was previously real estate editor for a group of 13 suburban newspapers.

Karina has personal experience in the property markets, including building a new home, renovating three homes and investing in a problem-laden but profitable one-bedroom apartment. She has also acted as a private consultant for several years, advising people on types of property and the locations in which to buy. Karina and her husband Stephen currently have three properties—two residential (inner-city and regional locations) and a suburban office.

Karina is also the author of a personal finance book titled *Surviving Tough Times* (Wrightbooks). She is listed in the *Who's Who of Australian Women*.

She has a diploma of financial markets and a certificate in financial planning principles and practice in Australia, as well as a diploma in journalism and diploma in editing from Massey University in New Zealand.

Karina and Stephen have a five-year-old daughter, Molly.

Bruce Brammall started as a cadet journalist with the *Herald Sun* in January 1992. After various rounds in the general newsroom, in 1999 he became an economics writer for the paper, where he focused on the lead-up to the introduction of the GST in July 2000. He then joined the *Herald Sun* business desk, where he has been the paper's chief reporter on banking, insurance, superannuation and wealth management. In 2003, he was made the deputy editor of *Business*, now *BusinessDaily*. He has written extensively on property purchase, financing and tax matters including for magazines such as *Display Homes* and *Auction*.

Bruce holds a bachelor of arts (communication), with a major in journalism. He also holds a diploma and an advanced diploma of financial services (financial planning).

Bruce married Genevieve in 2002. They live in Richmond in Melbourne, in a still only partly refurbished Victorian terrace built in 1885. They own three investment properties.

Chapter 1

The rewards of real estate

In this chapter we will cover the following:

▲ Who are property investors?

▲ Buying a home is also an emotional decision

▲ Why we all must invest for the future

▲ Why choose to invest in residential real estate?

▲ The risks and rewards of real estate

▲ Why home equity is important

▲ The tenant and the tax man can help your investment

▲ Commercial property

▲ Arming yourself with knowledge.

Australians love property. It has been the backbone of most family wealth since colonisation more than 200 years ago. Just take a look at the Aussie rich list each year and you'll soon see the number of millionaires and billionaires who have built their empires on real estate.

Property is embedded in the Australian psyche. 'The Great Australian Dream' is about buying the quarter-acre block with a freestanding home and, perhaps, having 2.3 kids playing in the backyard.

In reality, it's not always freestanding, it doesn't always have much land and it might be the place you escape to once the kids fly the coop. But it's all yours.

If only it didn't have to come with a mortgage.

Aha! But it doesn't always have to come with a mortgage. Of all the people living in houses, apartments, units, warehouses — you name it — throughout Australia, about two in three households don't have a mortgage.

That's right — only about one-third of people have a mortgage on the place in which they live. Another third once had a mortgage but have paid it off, while the remaining third pay rent.

Think about that for a second. On average, you can take any three homes anywhere in Australia and:

▲ The first house is owned outright by the people living there.

▲ The second house has a mortgage being paid off by the people living there.

▲ The third house has a tenant paying 'somebody else' so they can live there.

Our book is about the people who live in all three types of households. But predominantly it is about the 'somebody elses' and how you can become one of them.

These somebody elses are better known as property investors and own property for one reason — to secure a better financial future for themselves and their families. They believe investing in property to provide a home for a tenant to live in will make them money.

They believe that a better financial future might come from a passive income stream in the form of rent from the property or from buying, holding and selling property for a profit.

Whatever the aim, remember one-third of Australians pay somebody else to live in their property, which means there is an enormous opportunity out there for investors.

Who are property investors?

Who owns that one-third of property that is rented? Why do they own it?

Considering how much property is owned and rented out, you probably already know at least one property investor. It might be your parents, a sibling, a cousin or an uncle or aunt. Perhaps it's a friend, work colleague or someone you play sport with.

And there's a good chance you've heard them talk about it. Property investment has become one of the most popular topics for dinner party and barbecue conversations in Australia in the new millennium. Why? Well, because after being an underperforming asset class for much of the 1990s, property came roaring back to life with spectacular price rises in the late 1990s and early parts of this decade.

People have been stunned by the rise in value of their own homes over the past decade. Yet homeowners will listen transfixed when someone talks about their investment property. And many will simply boggle when a friend starts discussing a 'property portfolio'.

Property has always been a popular topic of conversation. Even people who have no real ambition to become investors still enjoy discussing the property market and its ups and downs. It has been one of the longest financial love affairs in Australian history.

And now, a lot of people have found themselves with enough equity in their family homes to make it possible to buy an investment property.

Property investment has helped make hundreds of thousands of property investors in Australia wealthier than ever.

Buying a home is also an emotional decision

The boom in the value of housing has given Australian homeowners an even greater sense of achievement. If they thought they got a bit of a bargain when they bought the house, then strong price gains will have reinforced that. But while the inner glow from the satisfaction of seeing your house price rise is nice, buying a home never has been, and never will be, just a financial decision.

Buying a home has an emotional aspect to it that is substantially different from someone paying rent to live in another person's property. A home, where you live, must also fulfill an emotional need. It must look right, it must cater to your family's needs and it must be in a location that suits you.

Buying an investment property is straight number crunching with no room for emotion. Yes, it must meet certain criteria, but these are to do with returns and tenant demand, not emotional needs or personal taste. While homes are not just financial assets, investment properties are just this.

Why we all must invest for the future

Property tends to be most people's biggest asset. By the time they retire, they hope to have paid off the mortgage — and getting to outright ownership is always a great achievement. But while a home will give you somewhere secure to live, it doesn't usually produce an income. And the utility bills, car registration, holidays, birthdays, clothes, groceries and telephone bills still keep rolling in.

When people stop working, their income usually comes from two sources — the government age pension or a private income from superannuation or other investments.

Who wants to rely on the government age pension as their sole or primary income source? Nobody, really. With the government setting it at 25 per cent of male average earnings, the government age pension can be a meagre existence with little or nothing left over most weeks. It is not enough to allow you to splurge on the children or grandchildren. Eating out at a reasonable restaurant will be a rarity. And you can forget expensive holidays.

The sad truth is most people fall well short of the income they hoped to have in retirement. For many people that means working longer than planned — or worse, never really being able to stop working — or settling for a lower income and trying to make ends meet.

....

Did you know?

In Australia in 2003–04, the average retired couple had net assets of $714 000, which included the value of their home. By that stage of life, 85 per cent of people owned their home and 4 per cent still had a mortgage. That meant approximately 11 per cent were still renting.

The average household income was $644 a week. At the time of the survey, the age pension for a couple was approximately $390 a week.

Source: Australian Bureau of Statistics

....

Why do so many people retire with so little? Largely, say the experts, because people don't plan for retirement until too late. It's easy to put off investing. There's the mortgage to pay, the kids to bring up, finally updating the car, or the much-needed holidays. It's only after these things have been paid for that people turn their attention to investing.

But the best time to start investing is now.

Why choose to invest in residential real estate?

Investment opportunities abound. There are simple interest-bearing investments, like bank accounts and bonds, and there are growth assets, like shares and real estate. Each investment option has its own characteristics. Each has a different risk associated with it and each has its own rewards.

So why choose property? Property has long been a favoured way for Australians to invest because it is a reasonably simple investment to understand — everyone needs a place to live. There will always be demand for rental housing because not everyone can afford to, or wants to, buy a home.

Property is easy to see. A house is a real object (unlike, say, the goodwill associated with the brand name of a company). It produces a regular income that will rise over the years and it usually produces a capital gain, which means a profit when it's time to sell.

It is an investment over which the investor can have as much or as little control as he or she chooses. You can be in control of where your investment is, who lives in it, and whether you want someone to manage it or whether you want to do it yourself.

Unlike shares in a bank, a property investor can also personally change a property. You can add value by renovating, redeveloping or simply giving it a quick makeover. A bank share is a bank share; you have no further input or control.

Property can also be about your future. An investment property can be a part of your lifestyle or future lifestyle — think holiday home or eventual retirement location.

But more importantly, property investment is about leverage. Finance lenders will lend more money to buy property than any other type of investment. They will often lend 110 per cent of the value of a property if there is another property as security; they consider it to be a much more stable investment than other investment options.

Because banks and lenders will lend more for property than, say, shares, you can invest a lot more money in property. Property investors, including people on modest incomes, can develop a portfolio of many houses over time. The advantage of having extra leverage is the ability to multiply gains when the value increases.

··

The power of gearing

Let's take two investors with $50 000 in savings. Both go to the bank and borrow money to invest. He wants to buy shares, and she wants to buy property. Because of the higher volatility associated with shares, the bank only lends about $100 000 to the shares investor, but could feasibly lend $250 000 to the property investor.

Over the next two years both shares and property increase in value by about 10 per cent each year. The share investor has seen his portfolio increase from $150 000 to $165 000, then to $181 500 — a gain of $31 500. The property investor,

The power of gearing *(cont'd)*

however, has seen her $300000 house increase in value to $330000 then to $363000 over the same period—a gain of $63000, which is double what the share investor made.

Imagine the potential over 10, 20 or 30 years!

Now consider what would happen if the property investor bought another investment property every few years, as the bank felt comfortable lending more money. If an investor has $1 million in property and the value of property increases by 10 per cent, that's a $100000 gain a year.

....

Another reason Australians are so fond of property is because property also has tax breaks. There are certain tax benefits — such as depreciation — that don't apply to all other investments that can add to property's attractiveness as an investment.

Have you heard of negative gearing? While negative gearing on its own is never a good reason to buy an investment, it can make sense for some investors to be negatively geared (see chapter 4 for more information).

And then there is the income stream. Rent not only helps pay for your investment in the early years when there is a mortgage, it also provides a valuable income stream for you to spend or live off once the mortgage is paid.

The risks and rewards of real estate

It's a fact — the main reason for owning investment property is to make money so that you can take control of your financial future. The money to be made from property comes from both income and capital gain.

But the primary rule of all investing is that risk and reward are linked. The higher the potential reward, the higher the risk. Property is no exception. Anybody who suggests otherwise is wrong. The risks in property investment mean that it may not be suitable for everyone.

Property prices do, sometimes, fall. There is a risk that when you go to sell you will not get as much money as you initially paid, resulting in a capital loss. This is most likely to occur when an investor decides to buy at the top of the market and has to sell after only a relatively short holding period, such as just a few years.

Most people who bought property during the property boom of 1989 to 1990 would have had to wait for many years — in some cases until the late 1990s — before property prices recovered and they could sell their property for the same price they had bought it for. In the most recent boom, the majority of investors who bought property in late 2003 or early 2004 in Sydney and Melbourne would have been unable to sell for a profit, even in 2006. Most other major capitals have continued to rise for some time after Sydney and Melbourne slowed (Perth and Darwin were still booming in mid 2006).

Another risk is that you will stop receiving rent. This could be either because a tenant refuses to pay or because you can't find a tenant. But you still have to pay the mortgage and it's much more difficult when there's no rent to help with the cash flow.

Also, property generally cannot be sold quickly. Selling usually takes some time. While technically it's possible to complete a sale within 30 days, most auctions have a sales 'campaign' that runs for a month or so before the property is sold. After that the buyer will often nominate a settlement or completion period of between 30 and 90 days, or sometimes longer. Houses for private sale can be on the market for several months before achieving an acceptable sale price. And in some cases, even after holding out for a couple of months, vendors may have to lower their expectations to get a sale.

Classic investment theory also says one investment property on its own lacks diversification. If you invest in only one property, then you are putting all your eggs in one basket. The risk here is that if property goes through a period of poor returns, the investor might have been better off having their money in other asset classes, or a mix of assets.

Property investment is not a dead certainty. There are risks. If the thought of these makes it difficult for you to sleep at night, then property investment may not be for you. But informing and educating yourself about risk usually helps put everything in perspective. So take the time to know as much as you can about property investment before you take the plunge.

Why home equity is important

Home 'equity' has become a real buzzword. It's in advertising slogans, it's splashed across the media and it seems everyone is talking about it. So what does it mean and why do we need home equity?

The term refers to how much of your home you actually own. You can get a good idea of how much equity you have quite simply: find out the value of your home and subtract the amount still owed on your mortgage. The difference is your equity. For example, a $400000 home minus the $200000 mortgage, gives you $200000 equity — or 50 per cent.

Equity is achieved in two ways — by paying off the mortgage and from an increase in the property value. Many people who bought a home five years ago or more will have achieved a bit of both. They will have made a small dent in the mortgage and also gained from an increase in property values.

Home equity can be used for many things, including helping you get into the real estate investment market.

Home equity is useful to you as a potential investor because it is what the bank prefers as security to minimise its risk. If someone has sufficient equity in their own home, the bank can be reasonably confident it can recoup its money if something goes wrong.

The tenant and the tax man can help your investment

If you remember back to signing on the dotted line to buy your first home, you'll probably recall it was pretty scary. Along with a place to call home came a huge commitment to a mortgage with an end date 20 or 30 years away. But after a few years, the mortgage fear may have become less daunting.

Investment property is a bit different in that you are not alone in paying the mortgage. You have two helping hands.

First, you have a tenant. The tenant pays rent and that usually covers a large part of the mortgage. In some cases, when a property becomes positively geared, it pays all of the mortgage and the other expenses as well.

Second, you have the tax man. The tax man helps by allowing you to claim back some of the ongoing losses if the income from the property does not cover all the expenses. He also allows you to claim depreciation — effectively giving you a cash return on the costs of fixtures and fittings (and in some cases the bricks and mortar itself) that are slowly wearing out.

Commercial property

Property is not a generic asset class. Residential real estate is about providing a home for someone to live in and for you to make a profit from doing that. The markets for two, three and four bedrooms are substantially different.

But commercial real estate is also an important part of this investment sector. Businesses need a home to live in too. Restaurants, car dealerships, fashion stores, banks, manufacturers, panel beaters, doctors, supermarkets — you name it — they all need a place to do business. And somebody also needs to own these properties.

The rules for commercial property are a little different from residential property, but the basic theory is the same. They both earn rental income and make capital gains. However, the lending rules for commercial property are usually different and you will need a bigger deposit. The potential returns from commercial property are higher than residential however, but so are the risks.

Arming yourself with knowledge

Our book is about arming you with the knowledge you need to step out into the world of property and secure your future through real estate.

In most cases, property investment is hands-on and you will be required to make regular decisions. To start with, you will need to decide where to buy, what to buy and how much to pay. But unlike shares or term deposits, you will also need to make ongoing decisions about how your property is maintained and managed. Although this can involve quite a lot of time, it also allows you to have control, something few other investments give you.

If you have started reading this book with the plan to do something about your financial future, then you have taken the right step. Property investment can be not only financially rewarding, but also personally rewarding, as in most cases you will have done the work or made the decisions yourself.

Chapter 2

Your home — the cornerstone of investment

In this chapter we will cover the following:

▲ Your home can be the cornerstone of your investment plans

▲ Renting versus buying

▲ Why there will always be people who want to rent property

▲ Purchasing a home is different from purchasing an investment property

▲ How to build equity in your home

▲ How to use equity to kick-start your investment plans

▲ Buying an investment property before buying a home.

Buying your first home is one of life's most exhilarating experiences. Emotions are involved. Many people reading this will remember that it can also be intimidating, if not downright scary. Buying a house is a huge commitment.

Do I really want to do this? Can I afford it? Am I ready for a 25-year loan commitment? Is this house, this street, this suburb, the best place for me?

Many people stumble with those questions. Some decide they don't really want to do it, they can't afford it or they don't want to live in that particular house, even if it is the only one they can afford. Some people never ask themselves these questions in the first place. Others are quite happy to rent.

Renting is less of a financial commitment. Renting often allows people to live in areas in which they couldn't afford to buy. And renting, as we'll show later in the chapter, is usually cheaper in the short to medium term.

This book does not assume everyone owns, or is paying off, their own castle. However, lots of you might have bought your first house a few years ago, a decade ago or longer. If you bought three to five years ago, perhaps you've made a bit of a dent in the mortgage by now, more so if you've made extra repayments. Those who bought 10 years ago might have raised their payments and paid off more than half by now. Others again might be considering buying their first property and will no doubt be making sacrifices for their savings campaign.

Your home can be the cornerstone of your investment plans

Strictly speaking, the home you live in is not an investment property. There are too many differences between 'homes' and 'investment properties'. The tax rules are different. The banks' lending rules are different. The reasons for buying a home (primarily to have a secure roof over your head) should be very different from those for buying an investment property (essentially an investment decision to make money). The purchasing decisions are different: 'Is this a place I want to live?' versus 'Is this a place tenants would want to live?' The way a property is treated is different—a fantastic tenant would treat the house even better if he or she owned it.

Your home is personal. You can do what you want when you want to (within council and legal limitations, of course). And while you can do a lot of what you want to an investment property, you can't while a tenant is living there.

However, while a home is not an investment property, it is the cornerstone investment decision most people will make in their life. It provides a solid foundation upon which financial decisions can be made later in life, including property investment.

A mortgage will eventually be paid off, giving you full ownership of your home, whereas rent never ends. Housing equity allows you to borrow money at a cheaper rate for, say, a car or a holiday. And, most importantly, a home can build equity (as the mortgage falls and the house's value rises) that will give banks security to lend money for other investments.

Banks, which have shareholders' interests to consider, are more likely to lend a large sum of money to someone with significant equity in his or her home than someone who doesn't own a home and has only ever rented. Why? Because if something goes wrong, the bank has the security of the equity to help make up any shortfall. In fact, some bank chiefs claim mortgages are 'almost riskless' for banks, especially if they also have lender's mortgage insurance.

Simply, banks will lend money to people with assets to back them up. It is clearly less of a risk to lend $300 000 to someone who owns outright a $500 000 home than someone who has no savings.

Renting versus buying

The forces that caused the property boom in Australia's eastern seaboard states—New South Wales, Victoria and

Queensland — in the late 1990s and early 2000s created an incredible imbalance in many sectors of the property market. Property, after a period of stagnation in the mid 1990s, was on a roll and investors were piling in. Prices were soaring and everyone seemed to be making money — or building equity — faster than expected.

But what happens when too many investors enter a property market? A bubble develops. And when the bubble deflates (as it has this time) or bursts (as it did in 1990), investors can get hurt. If there are more people selling properties in the market than there are buyers willing to purchase them, the price of property must fall. It's 'Economics 101' — supply and demand.

The same forces are at work in the rental market. If there are too many properties for rent, renters can be choosy and rent prices often stay stagnant or fall. This happened between 2001 and 2004. An excess of rental property meant there were few rent rises until the latter half of 2005, which led to renters' heaven. For example, in Melbourne in late 2005, when the average rent on a three-bedroom house was $270 a week, to buy the same house would have cost about $556 a week in mortgage repayments. The homebuyer would be paying $28 921 a year in mortgage repayments, while the renter was paying $14 040. That's a difference of nearly $15 000 to live in the same house.

'Experts' at the time said it made sense to rent in the short term, as long as the renters invested the difference ($15 000). How many people do you know who would have the strength or willpower to do that?

Fast fact

At any one time in Australia, approximately one-third of people rent, one-third have a mortgage and one-third own their home outright.

Those who believe renting is a sensible long-term strategy for saving money should think again.

There are several reasons for this. First, a mortgage has an end. Whether you choose a term of 25 or 30 years, it will eventually be paid off. Rent has no end. If you never buy, you will rent forever.

Second, part of the $15 000 difference between rent and the mortgage is principal repayment (or equity) being built in the home. In the first year of the mortgage the amount of principal repaid to the bank is about $5200. From there, the proportion of annual interest paid gradually decreases, while the principal paid increases. Many describe principal repayment as enforced savings.

Third, rents will rise roughly with inflation over the years. Mortgages will fluctuate with interest rates, but in real terms (after the effects of inflation), they tend to fall as the homeowner's income rises.

Here's how it works. There are two almost identical houses next door to each other. One was sold to a family we'll call the Buyer family, while the other was let to the Renter family. The houses are both valued at $341 000, which is what the Buyers paid.

As already stated, the Renters will be substantially ahead for the first few years. But their rent will increase over time with inflation, while the Buyers' mortgage will stay roughly the same.

By year 11, the Renters' rent will have risen to $18 869. They are still ahead overall, but the interest being paid by the Buyers is now only $18 437—less than the Renters are paying for rent—with the rest of the Buyers' mortgage repayments paying off the principal.

By year 25, the Buyers' mortgage is paid off. And the $28 921 they were paying to the bank each year becomes theirs to spend freely again. They own their $341 000 home outright.

The Renters, however, are still renting. Their rent has risen to $28540 a year. In year 30 they will be paying $33086 and in year 40 they will be paying $44465.

Forty years after the two families moved in, the Buyers are about $677000 better off (or $194000 with inflation). That does not include any increase in the house's value.

A graph that compares the differences between renting and buying is set out in figure 2.1, below (see the appendix for the data that the graph is based on).

Figure 2.1: renting versus buying

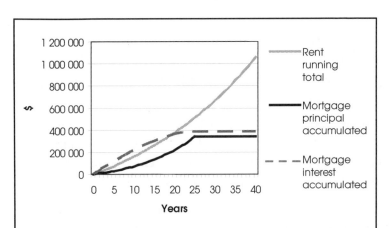

Our example has not factored in the Buyers' deposit or the expenses of home ownership. It has also used figures from one of the best periods for renters in recent times. Rents were very low in mid to late 2005. As we will show in the next chapter, rents in 2006 look to be playing catch-up and are rising by much more than the inflation rate of 3 per cent.

As some people argue, renting is indeed cheaper, but usually only in the short to medium term, particularly when repayments of principal — growing your equity — are included.

Why there will always be people who want to rent property

None of that is to suggest that people who choose to rent have lost their minds. Many tenants have equally compelling reasons for renting.

If what seemed like a nice place isn't such a nice place, you can easily and cheaply move (without paying any stamp duty). It is cheaper to rent in the short and medium terms. You can rent somewhere that you couldn't afford to have your own mortgage. If the hot-water service breaks, you don't have to pay for it. You don't have to pay the rates either. Gardening? No thanks!

There are other economic reasons. Many people might have only recently got their first job. Some are new to the city, or intend only to be there for a year or two. Others don't have the job security or simply can't afford to buy. Some intend to travel soon. Some have never had the urge to nest, but just wanted a place to 'store their stuff'.

There are also many people who do not have the security of owning a home as a priority—their interests or passions lie elsewhere. And there are, of course, those who are renting but are saving to buy.

Purchasing a home is different from purchasing an investment property

We mentioned earlier that the home you live in is not an 'investment property' for many reasons. But there is one reason we didn't mention earlier and it's arguably the most important of all—even though it seems so obvious.

The number one reason why an investment property is different from your home is that you are not going to live there!

It is a point too many people fail to grasp when they first start looking at investment properties, particularly those who have a 'home'. They walk into a potentially good investment property and say, 'Ooh, no, I wouldn't want to live here!'

You might not want to live there. That might be because it's too noisy. It's too close to a school. It's not close enough to a school. The bathroom is too poky. It's on a busy street. It's too close to or too far from the freeway. It's too inner-city. It's too outer-suburban. It doesn't have a garden. It does have a garden.

You might not want to live there, but that's not the point. The reason you don't want to live there might be the exact reason a tenant would want to.

Some people think tenants will live almost anywhere they can afford. There are some general rules about the sorts of amenities tenants want—and these are not necessarily dissimilar to what owner-occupiers want. Tenants generally like to be close to public transport, schools, shops and their workplace or at least a wide range of employment opportunities. They also want to feel safe, certainly within their own homes.

They are the important similarities. But what are the differences between tenants and owner-occupiers?

High-density living

Tenants seem keener than owner-occupiers to live in high-density dwellings (units and apartments). The rate of sales to investors of inner-city high-rise developments is much higher than to owner-occupiers, when compared with houses. Tenants also tend to be less interested in tending to a garden (not a major problem, as gardening services can be quite inexpensive and a tax deduction) although they may enjoy use of one.

Does it make apartments a good investment if tenants want to live in them? Not necessarily. Landlords who own apartments in large complexes compete for the same tenants and the apartment blocks usually have higher vacancy rates than low-density dwellings. Capital gains can be harder to achieve in high-rise buildings (particularly in inner-city areas) because there is a never-ending supply of apartments being built nearby. Why would renters pay $400 a week for a three-year-old apartment when they could rent a brand-new one for about the same price? It is more likely that the owner of the slightly older unit would have to drop the asking rent or the owner of the newer unit would have to increase his or hers.

Tax differences

When it comes to tax, a home and an investment are worlds apart. It almost seems unfair, but if you paid a tradesperson to do the same work on your home and your investment property (say, some gardening), the cost to you could be nearly twice as much for the work on your home as for the work on the investment property. Why? Because work on your investment property will generally qualify as a tax deduction. And that means the garden (or the newly repaired oven) your tenants are enjoying will be cheaper to give your tenants than to give yourself. If you spent $100 on gardening services for your home, that's how much it will cost you. However, if you spent $100 on gardening for your investment property, you will get back up to $46.50 back from the Tax Office, reducing the actual cost to just $53.50. For 'average' income earners (those who earned $25 000 to $75 000 in the 2006–07 financial year) paying 31.5 per cent as a marginal tax rate, the after-tax cost of that $100 gardener will be $68.50. (See chapter 9 for more details.)

Capital gains tax

The really big difference when it comes to your home versus your investment property is capital gains tax (CGT). Introduced in Australia in the mid 1980s, CGT is a tax on profits from selling investments.

If you buy an investment and sell it for a profit several years later—and that is one of the two main aims of investing, the other being a passive income stream from the rent—you must pay tax on a portion of your profit.

The rules have been tweaked over the years. Suppose you were to buy an investment property for $300 000 and hold it for longer than one year and then sell it for $400 000. You would have made a profit of $100 000. Under CGT rules at the time of writing, you would have to pay tax on only half your profit. That would mean adding $50 000 to your other income and then paying normal rates of tax on it.

There are exceptions to the CGT rules—and your home is one of them.

If you were to sell your home—or your 'principal place of residence', as the Tax Office calls it—you would pay no tax. You pay no tax if you make a profit of $100 000, nor if you make $1 million. That's a fairly big difference. CGT issues will be discussed further in chapter 14.

How to build equity in your home

So, if your home is not a true investment property, can it still help you build a wealthier future?

Absolutely! Remember, it is the cornerstone of investment, the foundation on which most people build themselves a more financially secure future. This is partially because homes are the cheapest source of finance available to most people (because, as explained before, banks feel more secure knowing that, if things go wrong, they will be able to regain the money loaned to you by selling the property).

A home is a great way to build equity because you can live in it and let it work for you to buy other investments. Equity is built in two ways—when you repay the money you borrowed (your mortgage) and when the value of your home rises.

Building equity

Let's say you bought your home three years ago. The house itself cost $280 000 and you had a 10 per cent deposit (plus your legal fees, including stamp duty), so you had a mortgage of $252 000. Over three years, the value of your home increased at 7 per cent a year and is now valued at $343 000. Sadly, because of the way principal and interest loans work, if you only made the minimum repayments, you would have only decreased your loan by $12 300 to $239 700.

However, there's still a significant improvement in your overall equity. When you first moved in, you had equity of $28 000. After three years of moderate growth and minimum repayments, you now have equity of $103 300 because of the rise in the value of the house to $343 000 and the slight reduction in the mortgage. In just three years, your equity has almost quadrupled.

And, of course, that figure would have grown further if you had made extra repayments.

Let's go back 10 years. The $343 000 house would have cost (assuming 7 per cent annual growth) approximately $174 000 and a 90 per cent loan would have been $156 600. The loan, with minimum repayments, would have reduced to $123 400. But your equity stake would be a whopping $219 600.

That's how equity is built—faster when house prices are galloping and slower when they are in a lull. If you can grasp the power this has with your own home, imagine how powerful it would be over time if you had not only your home, but also another investment property. Or two or three investment properties. Or a significant portfolio.

How to use equity to kick-start your investment plans

Banks are keen to help people access the equity in their homes. Why? Because lending is where banks make the majority of their money. And if an existing good customer with sufficient home equity wants another $100 000, it is much cheaper for a bank to lend to the existing customer than it is for the bank to go out and find a new customer who wants $100 000.

But beware, banks and other lenders often push, through advertising, for customers to access the equity in their homes for items like boats, new cars and holidays. Sure, you can do that. But boats, new cars and holidays are not going to create wealth. Most people know that a brand-new car loses something like 20 per cent of its value as soon as it's driven off the showroom floor. Holidays create wonderful memories — and they are a necessity for your sanity — but you won't have anything financial to show for your travels when you get back. These sorts of assets are commonly referred to as 'depreciating assets' because they decline in value. They are, in effect, wealth destroyers. Accessing the equity in your home should be used for what is known as 'good debt' as opposed to 'bad debt' or 'wealth destroying assets'.

We'd prefer to think that you're reading this book to create wealth through property. In other words, that you're buying 'appreciating assets', assets that should, in the future, give you the type of passive income — money that you have not had to do physical work to earn — that will help you pay for that holiday, buy that new car or have the nicest boat at the marina.

In essence, the building of equity happens naturally. Buy a house, pay the mortgage and meanwhile the house price should rise. It is what you do with that equity that becomes important.

Let's show, by way of example, how powerful equity can be for a couple who have owned their home for 10 years.

Example

The couple's house is worth $343000. They have a loan of approximately $123000 and equity of $220000.

They are interested in buying an investment property. They would like to spend about $300000 in total (including all their investment costs) buying a house on the other side of town (to diversify their property assets).

They buy a house for $280000. After the costs of stamp duty and legal fees, they will need a loan of approximately $300000.

From the bank's perspective, its client will have two properties worth about $623000 ($343000 for the home and $280000 for the investmentproperty). They will have debts of $423000 ($123000 plus $300000). Though they have negative equity in their investment property (the extra $20000 to cover legal costs), the bank will see that the couple still has equity of about $200000, or about 32 per cent.

The investors now have loans of $423000 instead of $123000. But they will also have a rental income to help meet the new mortgage, although probably not all of it. The tax man will also help with tax deductions and depreciation (these will be discussed in later chapters).

But, importantly, they will now have an investment property that will increase in value over time, plus their home. They have two houses worth a combined $623000.

Three years after the investment property purchase, their two properties are worth $763000 (assuming annual growth of 7 per cent). If they opted for interest-only repayments on the investment loan, their total debt would now be $108000 (at year 13 for the home loan), plus $300000 (on the investment), or $408000, a fall of $15000.

The net equity from their properties, however, would have risen to $355000, with the investment property — despite the huge loan — contributing approximately $43000.

Example (cont'd)

And then, perhaps, they might be ready to do it again. (We'll come back to this in chapter 10.)

Buying an investment property before buying a home

The most common way of becoming a property investor is to first buy your home, build some equity and then use that equity to help fund the purchase of an investment property. But it doesn't necessarily have to be that way. Increasingly, people are deciding to do the opposite. That is, buy the investment property first, then at some later stage use the investment property as an aid to move into the realm of home ownership.

It can be a good idea to get involved in an investment property if you are still living at home with your parents and don't really have any need or wish to move out. If mum and dad are happy to have you at home, then consider putting some of your savings to work by investing them. This could also save you money on your home purchase down the track. If you have built up equity in an investment property by the time you are ready to buy a home, then a bank will certainly look more favourably on any application you might make.

True story

Michael got all fired up about property investment after reading up on the topic in newspapers and financial magazines. He'd had some savings and hatched a plan immediately to buy a home, grow some equity and then get himself involved in another property investment.

But Michael's long-time girlfriend, Jenny, convinced him that he should wait until they could buy a home together. She was keen, but would need a year to save money herself.

Michael agreed to hold off on buying a home, but decided to plough some of his savings into buying an investment property in the mean time. He bought a unit for $141 000. Michael and Jenny then saved furiously for a year to buy their own home. By the time they went househunting, Michael's investment property had increased in value (according to the bank's valuation) to $170 000.

They bought a house for $336 000. They did not have enough deposit for the bank to waive charging them lender's mortgage insurance. But because the value of the investment property had risen by more than 20 per cent during the year, the amount of lender's mortgage insurance they were charged fell from about $10 000 to around $4000, saving them $6000 at the same time the equity in Michael's investment property had grown about $29 000.

A word of warning

Many people also make a conscious decision to buy an investment property with the intention of moving into it a few years later when a little of the mortgage has been paid off and some of the tax benefits involved with newer properties have diminished in value (this is discussed in chapter 9). There is nothing wrong with this as a strategy. However, you need to be aware that once a property changes from being an investment property to being a home, the taxation arrangements surrounding that property also change. Essentially, most things for which you could have claimed a tax deduction previously will not be claimable once it converts from an investment property to a home.

Further, when the house is later sold, a portion of any profit from the sale of the house will be CGT-free because it was a principal place of residence, but another portion of any profit will be subject to CGT.

For example, let's assume that a property was owned for 10 years before being sold for a $200 000 profit. For the first five years it was an investment property and for the second five years it was a family home (or vice versa). Half of the gains would be considered to be CGT-free because it was the family home. That would mean that the other $100 000 would have to be declared as a profit and would be subject to CGT rules.

Chapter 3

Assessing the returns

In this chapter we will cover the following:

▲   The risk–reward trade-off

▲   Investing in income assets or growth assets

▲   Property versus shares

▲   The different investment cycles

▲   The advantages of property

▲   Property investment income — rent

▲   Be prepared for periods with no rent

▲   Calculating your annual return.

Nobody wants to grow old and poor. But Australia's ageing population — caused by the first baby boomers retiring and not enough following generations available to take up the employment slack — puts the viability of the government age pension in doubt. And the age pension is at best a meagre existence anyway.

Considering you're reading this book, there's a good chance something has clicked to convince you that the single most important factor in determining whether you'll have to rely on the government down the track is your own actions — so take control of your financial future.

Property is a very powerful way of building wealth and securing your future. Because of the large amount of money involved in property — generally several hundred thousand dollars for each house — a relatively small move in value can mean a big move in actual price. How does that work? Well, if you had an investment of $50 000 and it increased in value by 10 per cent, the profit would be $5000. However, if you owned another investment worth $300 000 — the price for an average investment property — and its value increased by 10 per cent, the profit would be $30 000.

Imagine if you built a portfolio of three properties that was worth $1 million. If the value of those properties was to move 10 per cent in a year, that's $100 000 of additional profit. Now picture the profit from a string of properties worth $2 million!

That is the power of property — large sums of money multiplied by the force of compound growth to produce an impressive leveraging effect.

But it's also where the risk lies.

The risk–reward trade-off

Basic investment theory states that risk and reward are inextricably linked — to entice investors into taking a higher risk with their money, there must be potential for a higher reward. In investment terms, risk means there is a possibility some of the money (capital) you invested might be lost.

If 'Investment A' and 'Investment B' both offered potential profits of 6 per cent, but Investment B posed a greater risk, then Investment B would need to offer perhaps 8 per cent in potential profits to attract investors. And if there was an 'Investment C' that held more risks than A or B, then it would need to have the potential to return an even greater amount.

Investing in income assets or growth assets

There are four basic asset classes — cash, fixed interest, property and equities (also known as shares). Within each asset class there are a number of more specific investment types.

Cash and fixed-interest investments (loans to governments and businesses), are considered income assets. The return offered to the investor is usually interest income. There is not a lot of movement expected in the initial amount of capital invested.

An investor might put in $1000 and receive regular interest payments. When you want to make a withdrawal from a bank deposit, you can be pretty confident you will be able to get your full $1000 back. With fixed interest, when you go to withdraw and get your money back, you should also receive about $1000 (it might be a little higher or a little lower, but the amount should be similar). These asset classes tend to be for low-risk investors — those whose fear of losing any capital outweighs the need to increase it or earn greater returns.

Growth assets are different. Investors in property and shares are generally more interested in seeing the underlying value of their investment grow than in receiving a regular income from the investment. They don't necessarily seek high ongoing returns as much as investors in income assets do and are prepared to take the risk that the underlying asset — the property or the shares — will increase in value to make up for the income they are missing out on.

Unlike cash and fixed interest, growth-asset investors accept that occasionally the value of their capital investment might actually fall. However, over the long term, they expect bigger gains. Therefore, growth investors usually need to have longer investment time frames. In every five- or seven-year period, there could be a couple of negative years and investors in growth assets need to be able to ride out those bumps.

Long-term investment

American Warren Buffett, arguably the world's most successful investor, writes every year to the shareholders in his investment company, Berkshire Hathaway. Just months after the big 1987 stock market crash, when panic selling saw a quarter of the value of the stock market disappear, he wrote: 'Our favourite holding period is forever'.

Residential investment property is a growth asset. It should not be seen as a plan to get rich quick, no matter what some property spruikers claim. A property investor needs to be prepared to invest for many years.

Property versus shares

There are countless people who argue that shares outperform property in total returns. There are equally as many who swear by property's prowess. For every argument in favour of one, there is an equal argument in favour of the other. And each side is able to draw on statistics to prove its point. The problem with statistics is that they are easily manipulated. They present a version of the truth that the storyteller wants heard.

We do not want to ramp up property as the best-performing asset class and to denigrate shares as an investment. Over the long term (and we're talking decades), both asset classes are expected to perform well.

Notable quote

There are three kinds of lies: lies, damned lies, and statistics.

Benjamin Disraeli, twice prime minister of the United Kingdom.

Asset performance data compiled by the Australian Stock Exchange and investment house Russell shows that the combined performance of Australian shares over the 10 years to December 2005 was 11.8 per cent a year. The average for residential investment property was 12.1 per cent, while Australian listed property was even higher with a 14 per cent annual return. This shows they are all in the same ballpark.

Sadly, as has long been complained about, the availability of up-to-date and reliable figures on Australian residential property markets is atrocious. You can look at the stock market and get up-to-the-minute information every day. But between the various agencies that collect data on residential property, even where the data is reasonably reliable, it is at best many months old.

However, we can say that the average price for a detached dwelling in Australia, according to the federal Treasury, increased from $148 000 to $358 000 between 1983 and 2003. That represents a compound return of 4.5 per cent; however, it does not include the rental income that would have been earned by the investor over that period. Between 1983 and 1993, the average gross yield was 7 to 8 per cent, while in the 10 years to 2003, it averaged 5 per cent (but hit a low of around 3 per cent in 2003 before it started to recover). The residential property figures are not directly comparable for a number of reasons, including that the costs of upkeep of the properties are not included.

One thing that can be stated with certainty is that property prices have much lower volatility. The price of an individual company's shares can rise or fall by 10 or 20 per cent (or occasionally more) in a day. An index like the All Ordinaries or New York's Dow Jones Industrial Average can fall dramatically in just one day or even hours. They can also rise pretty fast.

Property tends not to behave like that. It can rise and fall quickly — but not overnight like shares. In fact, property assets tend to have about half the volatility of shares over extended periods.

Volatility measures the bumps in the road. Shares are a true roller-coaster — their value can go up and down each time they are traded, which can be every minute. Property, on the other hand, doesn't have the highs or lows and tends to be a smoother ride. Property is heading in the same direction as shares, but its path is not so dramatic.

That property is usually a nice, steady ride is really appealing to many property investors. It has a fairly dependable income stream and, unlike individual companies, it has a much lower chance of becoming worthless overnight. Even if the house burns down and the tenant can no longer pay rent, there is always the value of the land (and, with adequate insurance, both the house and the rent would be covered). The land value of houses can be as much as 60 per cent of the value of the property. Even in high-rise properties with dozens or hundreds of units, the land still has some value.

The different investment cycles

All investment classes have cycles — periods where they perform differently from other investments. If property is running hot, the sharemarket might not be. Or if the Australian sharemarket is doing well, then perhaps international markets aren't.

That is also true of sectors within investment classes. In the stock market, bank shares have been consistently strong performers following a period of instability in the early 1990s. Mining shares have come into their own since late 2003, when resource companies soared on the back of huge demand for their products from China. At the same time, there are other stocks — notably Australia's most widely held stock, Telstra — that have been going backwards, despite Australia being in its strongest sharemarket boom ever.

Even cash has cycles! Australian cash cycles are largely determined by what the Reserve Bank of Australia (RBA) is doing with interest rates. If the RBA is raising interest rates, cash returns rise; if the RBA is reducing interest rates, cash returns fall.

Property is not a homogenous product. It has many sectors. Just because prices move in Sydney does not mean that prices are also shifting across the Nullabor in Perth.

Melbourne and Sydney benefited from a recent property boom that started in the late 1990s and continued until late 2003. Queensland was not far behind. But other states came to the property party a little later. Now the markets of Australia's two largest cities have fallen from their 2003 peaks, but other capitals, including Perth and Darwin, are continuing to enjoy strong growth into 2006 (and are forecast to continue into 2007), partly because they have different economic fundamentals.

The Western Australian market is a particularly good example of an economy operating on different fundamentals to the rest of the nation and how that can affect property prices. The global resources boom started in 2003 and Western Australia, more than any other state, has been a benefactor. Western Australia's vast outback holds an enormous amount of the minerals, resources and fuels that the powerfully growing nations — the BRIC countries, or Brazil, Russia, India and, most importantly, China — need.

The demand for commodities has seen jobs and money pour into Western Australia's economy. In mid 2006, when property prices were flat in the eastern states, Perth was experiencing double-digit growth.

Property prices don't always rise. They sometimes fall and can fall hard for several years — Sydney's prices fell 25 per cent during the property crash of the late 1980s and early 1990s, while Melbourne's fell about 10 per cent over a similar period. At other times, they may stay fairly stable for years at a time. But it's important to remember each sector can act differently.

The advantages of property

So, if the annual performances of property and shares are in the same ballpark, why choose to invest in property? There are many good reasons, including:

▲ Property is an investment concept that is fairly easy to understand — if you own a house, you already know a little about property.

▲ Property is an investment you can see, feel and touch, which can be difficult with some investments on the stock market.

▲ You have some control over your property, unlike owning a few shares in a large company.

▲ There will always be tenants, so property will always be in demand.

▲ You can be involved in running your property yourself (or you can pay others to do some of the work).

▲ Property can be renovated to improve the value.

▲ Some properties can double as holiday homes.

However, there is one thing that differentiates property from other assets as a pure investment — a higher level of gearing.

Banks lend a lot of money for property. Banks feel comfortable lending money for property. They've done it for hundreds of years. Residential real estate is the number one business of most of Australia's banks, building societies (their name comes from property lending) and credit unions. Property has made banks the multibillion-dollar organisations that they are. And, in many cases, it has made their customers wealthy with them.

Banks have always been prepared to lend their customers more money for residential real estate than for anything else. Go into your bank and ask the branch manager for $300 000 to buy your first home and, if you've saved a reasonable deposit and you're a reasonable character, it will give it to you. If you become a good customer and you go back five years later asking for another loan to buy an investment property, your bank will probably say yes again.

Why? Banks have enough experience with property (and lending to home buyers) to have developed confidence in the industry. True, sometimes banks get burnt by lending to the wrong people, or lending too much to the wrong sectors at the wrong time. But banks are confident in property because it is not a volatile asset. They also have the security of having a valuable asset if a problem arises with the mortgagee or investor.

Banks aren't guaranteed the same level of security when it comes to lending on businesses (whether family-run or large businesses or corporations) or shares, even in blue-chip companies.

More evidence of the confidence of banks in residential real estate includes:

▲ Banks set their interest rates according to the risks associated with that type of loan — residential property mortgages are lowest, followed by business loans, car loans and credit cards.

▲ Banks will lend up to 95 per cent of the value of a first home, but offer much lower percentages for business or car loans.

▲ When backed by other security, banks will lend up to 110 per cent of the value of an investment property (to cover property expenses incurred in addition to the property price).

▲ Banks will usually lend only 70 per cent for commercial property.

▲ Banks will usually lend only about 70 to 80 per cent for margin loans for share trading accounts (although possibly more if backed by residential property).

In fact, banks will lend a lot more money for anything if the loan is backed by property. That's why people who have equity in their homes are regularly offered more money from banks.

This can often mean that people with fairly modest incomes from their day jobs can sometimes have loans of more than $1 million (and even multimillion-dollar loans in many circumstances).

Borrowing to buy investment property, which is known as gearing or leveraging, allows an investor to get a much larger exposure to an asset class. Imagine how long it would take to save enough cash to buy a $250 000 investment property. By gearing, investors can use a much smaller amount of money (or none if they wish to back it with the equity in their home) to buy a sizeable asset such as an investment property.

Gearing is a major force behind the power of property and will be discussed in detail in the next chapter.

Property investment income — rent

Investment is not all about making big capital gains. A big consideration in any investment strategy should be income — and many property strategies are based on rent as the income. That is, the intention is that down the track (in perhaps 20 years) the investment loan taken out for the property will be negligible or gone and the rent will continue to flow in. Not only do the investors own this valuable asset, but it is now paying them money every month. And, over time, the rent paid should rise to at least keep pace with inflation.

In recent years, rents have gone through long periods of stagnation. Like property prices, rents are determined by demand and supply. The Real Estate Institute of Australia (REIA) reported that rents had finally started to rise in most states of Australia in the last quarter of 2005, after four years of little or no growth.

Rents stayed low from 2001 to 2004 for two reasons. First, there were a lot of investors buying properties and offering them for rent. This gave potential renters more choice. When potential tenants have lots to choose from, they can bargain with agents or even play them off against each other to drive down the price. Second, particularly until the 'affordability' crush kicked in, those people who previously rented started buying houses to live in. That meant there were more properties to rent but a smaller pool of people wanting to let them.

There is no magic number for vacancy rates, but it is generally accepted that a vacancy rate of about 3 per cent represents a rough equilibrium. It means about three in every 100 properties are vacant at the time of counting. This can also be roughly translated by saying that if a house became vacant, it would, on average, be without a tenant for about 3 per cent of a year, or one and a half weeks. Landlords will generally be able to fill their houses within a few weeks of them being vacated and they won't feel the need to drop their rents to attract a tenant. At 3 per cent, there is sufficient variety on offer for tenants and rents will probably rise in line with inflation.

If vacancy rates go below about 2.5 per cent, or above 3.5 per cent, an imbalance is created. Below 2.5 per cent and landlords have a lot of demand for their properties and can push rents higher. Above 3.5 per cent and renters can be choosey, so rent prices are likely to stay stagnant, or perhaps even fall. The period between 2001 and 2004 was a good time for tenants. There were plenty of places to rent and no pressure for prices to rise.

But that period appears to have come to an end.

....

Vacancy rates and their effect on rents—the year to March 2006

At the time of the REIA's March 2006 property survey, the tightest rental market in Australia was Perth, with vacancies of just 1.4 per cent. This was probably a result of workers flocking to the area for the plentiful and highly paid jobs available in the booming mining sector. The cost of renting a three-bedroom house in Perth in the year to March 2006 rose by 20 per cent, to $240 a week. An even stronger demand for two-bedroom apartments saw weekly rents rise by 29.4 per cent, to $220 a week.

Like Perth, Brisbane's vacancy rate was also very tight in the year to March 2006, at just 1.5 per cent, but demand was less explosive. In Brisbane, rents for three-bedroom houses increased by a modest 6.3 per cent, to $255 a week; although, interestingly, two-bedroom units had an 11.1 per cent boost to $250 a week.

At the time of the survey, Adelaide had a vacancy rate of 1.7 per cent. In Adelaide the cost of renting a three-bedroom house was 6.8 per cent higher than in the previous year, with rents rising to $235 a week in 2006. However, two-bedroom units were the better performers, with weekly rents up 8.8 per cent, to $185.

With a vacancy rate of 1.8 per cent in March 2006, Melbourne and Canberra saw a higher vacancy rate than Adelaide.

Melbourne houses and apartments showed more modest rental growth, with weekly rents increasing by 4.5 per cent. However, it's worth noting that three-bedroom houses and two-bedroom apartments earned the same rent of $230 a week — an unusual situation given the lower purchase price of the smaller apartments.

In Canberra, in the year to March 2006, weekly rents for houses nudged up 3.3 per cent, to $310. Apartments did better, with a rent rise of 7.1 per cent and weekly rents of $300.

Sydney had a low vacancy rate of 2 per cent but only managed a poor 1.9 per cent rent increase for houses, while apartments were little better at 3.4 per cent. And, similar to Melbourne, two-bedroom apartments outperformed three-bedroom houses, despite the big purchase-price difference. Two-bedroom units in Sydney generated rents of $300 a week, while three-bedroom houses only earned $265 a week.

At March 2006, Darwin had the highest vacancy rate, at 3.3 per cent; however, rents in this market still performed better than some of the cities with lower vacancies. Three-bedroom houses in Darwin demonstrated an 11.1 per cent increase for the year, with weekly rents at $300, while two-bedroom apartments went up 10 per cent, to $220.

Hobart's vacancy rate of 2.2 per cent saw three-bedroom house rents increase by 8.7 per cent, to $250, while two-bedroom units were the better performers, showing rent increases of 15.9 per cent, to $197 a week.

Be prepared for periods with no rent

It happens to all investment properties — the onset of periods where the mortgage still has to be paid, but there's no rent coming in to help meet the monthly payments.

Residential tenants tend to sign leases for 6 or 12 months. The majority of the time, investors will be happy to let a tenant stay on indefinitely, so long as the rent is paid and there aren't too many concerns raised with the regular inspections. In fact, they are the ideal tenants — those who consistently pay the rent on time, treat the property like it is their own and who never want to leave!

But tenants staying on indefinitely doesn't happen often — it is more likely that tenants will move on after a year, or perhaps two or three years.

It can take a while to find new tenants when the old ones leave. Sometimes it only takes a few days. More often than not, it will take at least a week or two, but it can take up to a month or longer. If it does take a long time, the investor might choose to drop the rent until a tenant sees it as a bargain. While this will hurt financially, trying to pay a large mortgage with no rent at all can hurt more.

Handy hint

When doing your calculations, it is safer to work out your numbers based on the property being vacant for about two weeks a year.

Calculating the annual return

The amount of rent you receive determines whether your property is positively, neutrally or negatively geared.

Rents are set by the market. An investor who tries to rent out a unit for $380 a week, when there is a similar unit nearby for $300, is unlikely to get the price he or she is seeking. Even if the $300-a-week house lets quickly, tenants are likely to pay $320 for another house nearby before they fork out $380 a week for a clearly overpriced house. To use an economist's term, renters tend to operate in a 'well-informed market'. It only takes a quick look at an agency's rental list, or a peek on the internet, to determine a reasonable price for the area.

Therefore, before you buy a property, it is imperative you get some idea of what properties in the area rent for. This can be done easily on the internet, but valuable information can be gained as you look for investment properties.

Ask agents to quote what a particular property is likely to rent for (banks often want this information in writing from agents anyway for loan approval). While selling agents often have little idea about the rental market, they will be happy to organise a colleague who specialises in the rental market to assess it for you — anything for a sale.

Have a look at a few places yourself while wandering between 'open for inspections'. You will often find you have some spare time between appointments, so make time to drop in on a few rental 'opens'.

Investors want to know what their investment return will be. And while we promise not to introduce too many formulas into this book, the following is important to be able to compare properties within a similar area. It is quite a useful tool to maximise your earnings or (if negatively geared) to minimise your ongoing losses. It is a formula used by professional analysts for shares and commercial properties, which applies equally to residential-investment property investors. The formula is as follows:

$$\text{Annual return} = \frac{\text{annual rent}}{\text{purchase price}}$$

Example

For a house purchased for $270 000 that could be rented for $240 a week, the equation would look like this:

$$\text{Annual return} = \frac{\$240 \times 52}{\$270\,000} = \frac{\$12\,480}{\$270\,000} = 4.62\%$$

Obviously, properties sell for different prices and attract different rents. But this relatively simple formula will provide you with a useful tool to compare properties. That is not to say that the highest returning property will be the best. But, particularly in the early stages of building your property portfolio, it will help you get an idea of how positively (or negatively) geared your investment property is.

Fast fact—the 5.2 per cent rule

A property bought for a figure where the weekly rent is one thousandth of that purchase price is a property with an annual return of 5.2 per cent. To work it out, take the last three zeros off the purchase price. For example, $280 a week is one thousandth of $280000, and $430 a week is one thousandth of $430000.

It won't happen often that it will be exact, but it is a quick rule for knowing how close a property is to returning 5.2 per cent a year.

Determining the annual return allows an investor to compare properties that might not have much in common. Let's see how this can be used to sort out a few different properties.

Example

During a weekend of property hunting, you find four three-bedroom properties in different areas of the same suburb.

Property 1

Expected sale price: $320000

Expected rental: $290 a week

Older house on big block, has off-street parking for two cars. It needs repainting.

Property 2

Expected sale price: $330000

Expected rental: $340 a week

Small block with no garden to speak of, but good public transport access to university.

Property 3

Expected sale price: $290000

Expected rental: $290 a week

Bigger than property 2. Very close to two primary schools.

Property 4

Expected sale price: $360000

Expected rental: $320 a week

Large two-year-old unit with one off-street park.

Let's look at the table below to compare the annual return of each of these properties.

Property	Sale price	Weekly rent	Annual rent	Annual return (%)
1	$320000	$290	$15080	4.71
2	$330000	$340	$17680	5.36
3	$290000	$290	$15080	5.20
4	$360000	$320	$16640	4.62

What does this tell you? Clearly, the highest return, from a rental perspective, is property 2, followed by properties 3, 1 and 4. It does not mean property 2 is the best property, but it does give you one more thing to compare. High returns should never be the sole reason for deciding to purchase, but they do help.

When you are buying an investment property, it is important to remember that you are not buying the property to live in it. You are buying it for other people—tenants—to live in. What do tenants want? That will vary from suburb to suburb and town to town, but if the property is in a suburb with young families, then schools will be important. If it is in the inner city, then perhaps restaurants are important to your potential young professional renters. It pays to think about the area that you're buying into.

Chapter 4

Gearing up for your first investment property

In this chapter we will cover the following:

▲ What is gearing?

▲ The different types of gearing

▲ Why losing money through negative gearing can still be worthwhile

▲ The obvious benefits of positive gearing

▲ In whose name should the investment be made?

Gearing is a term everybody has heard, but not everybody understands. And how about negative gearing? Positive gearing? They are common phrases tossed around in the investment pages of newspapers and magazines, but what are they? How would they affect an investment decision that you're about to make?

What is gearing?

Gearing is simply another name for using borrowed money to make larger investments than you could with your own savings. It gets its name from gears, like those on a bicycle. In first gear, a cyclist's legs will have to pedal quickly to move even fairly slowly, say, at 15 or 20 kilometres per hour. But as you move up the gears, from first to fifth and on to tenth, fewer turns of the pedals are required to move significantly faster, at, perhaps, 50 kilometres per hour.

When it comes to investing, staying in first gear is the equivalent of using only *your* money. If you put $1000 in an investment and the investment increases in value by 20 per cent, then it is now worth $1200, and you have made $200.

If you move into second gear, perhaps you would use your own $1000 and then borrow $1000 to have $2000 to invest. If the investment improves by 20 per cent again, then it is now worth $2400. You have $400, twice as much than if you had only used your own money.

If you are in 10th gear, you might put your $1000 into an investment along with $9000 in borrowings, making a total investment of $10 000. If the market then improves 20 per cent, your investment will rise to $12 000 and you will have made $2000, or 10 times more than when in first gear.

Gearing exaggerates movements. It allows investors to have a much larger exposure to a market, be that property or the sharemarket, and exposure is one of the keys to property investment.

Because gearing exaggerates results, it will exaggerate on the downside as well as the upside. If the value of the investment in first gear falls by 20 per cent, the investor's capital will fall from $1000 to $800 — a loss of $200.

Gearing can lead to quite severe losses, where investors lose all their own money and potentially some of the bank's money.

For example, if there is a 20 per cent fall in the value of the 10th-gear investor's asset, his or her $10 000 investment will fall to just $8000. If the investment then has to be sold, the investor will lose not only the initial $1000, but $1000 of the bank's money as well, which will still have to be repaid.

Gearing, therefore, is considered a high-risk investment strategy. But, in the same way that few people are able to buy their first home in cash, investment property is largely bought with borrowed money. Borrowing involves paying interest, so you should aim to only borrow money to invest in assets where there is a good chance the income or capital gain from the property will exceed the costs of the loan (if not immediately, then in the foreseeable future).

The different types of gearing

Borrowing money isn't for everybody. Some people actually fear debt. And through what some sociologists call 'learned behaviour', children often adopt their parents' attitudes to debt. If mum and dad had trouble dealing with money, there's a good chance their children will pick that up and take it with them through life.

A fear of debt actually 'works' for some people. As a result, they pay for everything with cash or a debit card and never buy a house because, to them, owing a bank money for 25 years is a scary commitment that they can't or don't want to make. These people will often be happier renting, because it is both reasonably cheap and, for them, a better option than a seemingly never-ending home loan.

Other people are comfortable only with small amounts of debt, like a credit card or a car loan. Then there are those who will take out a loan to buy a house, but want to pay the loan off quickly — no more debt for them. Then there are investors who understand that debt *can* be a wealth-creating tool. Property investors tend to be in this space, and have long-term goals and a preparedness to take on some risks to secure their future.

But even among property investors, there are different types of debt personalities. They tend to correlate with the types of gearing — positive, negative and neutral. You can probably get an idea of your own personality by assessing which description of gearing you feel most comfortable with.

This leads us to the three types of gearing — positive, negative and neutral.

Positive gearing

Positive gearing is where the income from the investment more than covers the costs of the investment. When talking about property, the income is usually from one source — the rent. But the costs are numerous; they include interest, insurance, rates, agent's fees, letting fees, advertising and maintenance.

Let's say the rent received for a property is $300 a week ($15 600 a year). If you paid $10 000 in interest for the year, plus $500 in rates, plus $500 in insurance, $1000 in agent's fees and another $500 for other expenses, your total costs would be $12 500. You are ahead by $3100 and drawing an income from the property. In this case, the net income of $3100 would be declared as income and tax would have to be paid on it. This is positive gearing.

Negative gearing

The opposite of this is negative gearing. It occurs when the costs of the investment are higher than the income. Let's again assume rent of $15 600 a year. While the rest of the costs (agent's fees, insurance, rates, etc.) remain at $2500, a larger amount was borrowed and the interest cost is $17 500 a year, making total costs of $20 000. In this case, the investor has $4400 more in expenses than has been received in income, meaning there is an ongoing cashflow 'loss'. This is an example of a negatively geared property.

Neutral gearing

Neutral gearing is the area in the middle of positive and negative — where an investor neither makes money, nor loses it. In reality, a neutrally geared property — where rent exactly equals all your other costs — is highly unlikely. So, in a broad sense, a neutrally geared property is generally considered to be one where the gain or the loss is within about $1000 or $2000.

Example

Let's look at how you can have a neutrally geared property. We'll assume you put in $100000 of a property's $315000 total cost.

	Income	Expenses	
Rent	$18200		
Agent's fees (8%)		$1456	
Insurance		$700	
Rates		$700	
Maintenance		$1000	
Subtotal	$18200	$3856	
Interest ($215000 at 7%)		$15050	
Total	$18200	$18906	
Total loss	$18200 −	$18906	= $706

This is essentially a neutrally geared property, because after that $706 is claimed against your other income, your loss could be as little as $7.26 a week (using the 46.5 per cent tax rate). And when depreciation is considered, you could possibly become positively geared.

Why losing money through negative gearing can still be worthwhile

It doesn't seem quite right that an investor would deliberately lose money on an investment. But there are reasons, or circumstances, where this might make sense. In Australia, losses on an income-producing investment (like real estate and shares) can reduce your other income. Therefore, if a property investor earning $70 000 made an investment loss of $4400, the Tax Office would allow the investor to deduct that sum, effectively reducing his or her taxable income to $65 600. The lower income means there will be less tax to pay. For example, the difference between the tax paid on $70 000 and $65 600 is $1386 (based on a marginal tax rate of 31.5 per cent), which for most people becomes a tax return. The extent of the 'loss' from the investment would then be reduced to $3014 — the initial $4400 minus the tax return of $1386.

Example

Let's see how this might work. Our example investment property is purchased for $300 000. It rents for $350 a week. The fixed costs total $3856.

We'll assume the current interest rate to be 7 per cent. If you had borrowed the entire value of the property plus your extra costs (stamp duty and legals, for example), you might have borrowings of $315 000. An interest-only loan is going to cost you $22 050. Add the interest costs to your other costs and you have total costs of $25 906.

	Income	Expenses	
Rent	$18 200		
Agent's fees (8%)		$1 456	
Insurance		$700	
Rates		$700	
Maintenance		$1 000	
Subtotal	$18 200	$3 856	

	Income	Expenses	
Interest ($315 000 at 7%)		$22 050	
Total	$18 200	$25 906	
Total loss	$18 200 –	$25 906	= $7706

Technically, the loss is $7706, but the ATO will allow you to reduce any other income by $7706, reducing the tax you have to pay. You could get a tax refund on that loss of up to $3583.29 (if on the top rate of 46.5 per cent). This would bring the total 'loss' down to $4122.71 ($7706 – $3583.29). If you were on the 31.5 per cent tax rate, your $7706 loss would generate a tax refund of $2427.39, reducing the overall cost from $7706 to $5278.61. (In most cases the loss will be further reduced by depreciation. See chapter 9.)

If being negatively geared means that investors are losing money, you may wonder why you should ever go ahead with the investment. But remember that while you are losing money in the short term, capitals gains will, with any luck, make up for that loss in the long term.

People with negatively geared investments generally hope for two things; the first is that the underlying value of the investment will rise faster than the ongoing losses. That is, if the investor is losing $4400 a year on the property, but the property increases in value by 10 per cent from $300 000 to $330 000, then the capital gain of $30 000 is a win. This does not always happen, but it is the risk that investors who negatively gear are prepared to take.

The second hope is a gamble that, over time, the rent will rise — and the interest costs for the mortgage will reduce — to the point that the property becomes neutrally or even positively geared. If the rent for the negatively geared house rises from $300 to $385 a week ($20 000 a year), and the total costs for the year are the same ($20000), the investment will be neutrally geared. A further few years and it will probably be positively geared.

That's the theory. Inflation ensures rents rise over time, and while rents will not rise uniformly with inflation, they should keep pace over the long term.

The obvious benefits of positive gearing

Some property investors swear by positive gearing — earning a positive income from your investment from day one. This can be achieved in one of two ways. One is that you buy a house that has high annual rent, but you buy it at a low price. Depending on where the market is in the property cycle, these properties tend to be in regional and rural towns or, sometimes, in outer-metropolitan areas.

The other way of buying a positively geared property is to put up enough of your own cash as a deposit so the ongoing costs of the property (such as interest, council rates, insurance and agent's fees) are less than the rent.

....

Example

Let's take the example of a negatively geared property purchased for $300000, with total costs taking that amount up to $315000. We'll assume you put in $135000. (See table opposite.)

Now you have a positive income of $1744, which will be added to your regular income. If you are on the lowest marginal tax rate (0 per cent), you might not pay any tax. If you are on the highest tax rate (46.5 per cent), you could lose up to $810.96 of that income.

(Again, depreciation, if applicable, could improve the situation — see chapter 9.)

	Income	Expenses	
Rent	$18 200		
Agent's fees (8%)		$1 456	
Insurance		$700	
Rates		$700	
Maintenance		$1 000	
Subtotal	**$18 200**	**$3 856**	
Interest ($180 000 at 7%)		$12 600	
Total	**$18 200**	**$16 456**	
Total profit	**$18 200** –	**$16 456**	**= $1744**

This last case is just one of many that can lead to a positively geared property. A positively geared property gives the investor 'passive income' — income that the investor just sits back and waits for. Most long-term investors aim to create a passive income stream to secure their future.

The other way a property can be positively geared is by buying a property where the rent is relatively high and the purchase cost is relatively low. But these properties have become harder to find following the most recent property boom. It is very difficult to find quality houses in inner-metropolitan areas that offer the potential for positive gearing and they are only marginally easier to find in outer-metropolitan areas.

Some property experts who focus on positively geared portfolios say these properties can still be found in larger regional areas and smaller rural towns. However, as a general rule, the higher the rental return, the more likely it is there could be long periods without tenants. Why? It's about supply and demand of tenants and investment risk. Small towns tend to have fewer drawcards (like employment or education) to keep a flow of tenants coming through, as compared with, say, a capital city. Due to this risk, investors tend to discount the purchase price they will pay for an investment in non-metropolitan areas.

The important thing to remember about positive gearing is that it tends to occur naturally over time. Why? Because rents usually rise while the interest component on the mortgage falls (as the principal is repaid).

Example

Let's look again at the example used earlier, but move forward 10 years. Say rents increased by a little more than inflation—4 per cent a year. At the end of that 10th year, the rent should have risen from $350 a week to about $518 a week. Now take the negative-gearing example in which you had borrowed for the total costs of the property ($315000). Assuming the principal has not been repaid at all, this is what the returns will now look like:

	Income	Expenses	
Rent	$26936		
Agent's fees (8%)		$2154	
Insurance		$700	
Rates		$700	
Maintenance		$1000	
Subtotal	$26936	$4554	
Interest ($315000 at 7%)		$22050	
Total	$26936	$26604	
Total profit	$26936 −	$26604	= $332

In the negative-gearing example (with the same $315000 borrowings), the annual loss was $7706. The rising rent has turned it into a property that is now positively geared to the tune of $332. This is a rough example that hasn't taken into account increased expenses (apart from the agent's fees), but it also hasn't taken into account the potential for lower interest costs if some principal has been repaid.

In whose name should the investment be made?

If you're looking to buy your first investment property, in whose name should the title be placed? And should the name on the title be influenced by whether the property is positively or negatively geared?

When it comes to investment property, you are usually signing up for a second (or third or fourth) debt of hundreds of thousands of dollars. In return you hope to get a regular income (rent) and you are also hoping to make a nice capital gain later when you sell.

Ownership of the investment is therefore a very important decision. Ongoing ownership considerations, including tax, are a large part of harnessing the power of property. Ownership options for single people are limited — you will probably need to buy in your name only (unless you are buying through a company or a trust, which is beyond the scope of this book). For couples, there are a number of options. One partner could own it or it could be jointly owned. It is also possible in some states to own it in portions (say 30 per cent in the name of the husband and 70 per cent in name of the wife).

Shared property ownership

However, no investment decision should be made for tax reasons alone. It should only be one part of a complete decision-making process.

More and more Australians are buying investment property through syndicates or family groups. This is a popular way for a small group of people to purchase a property that they might not be able to afford as individuals.

Parents and children are the biggest group buying property jointly — some lenders report that more than half their joint borrowers are mum and/or dad and one or more of the kids. Siblings and other extended family members are also getting in on the act, as well as groups of friends and even work or social club colleagues. Each person, of course, will have his or her own tax situation, so the division of profits or debt (negative gearing) needs to be based on the amount of equity and ongoing contributions made.

However, if you're considering this type of ownership, the most important tip a lawyer will give you is to establish your exit strategy first. As with any partnership, business or personal, you don't enter the arrangement expecting it to end badly, but, unfortunately, in many situations that is exactly what happens.

Every shared-property ownership arrangement should also include a detailed, step-by-step process about how to exit the arrangement or the action that needs to be taken when only one owner wants out. The agreement should include details about:

▲ how the property will be valued

▲ how much notice the other partners must be given

▲ who can buy the available share

▲ what happens to the profits

▲ how the costs are divided

▲ what happens if one person doesn't pay his or her way.

The list is substantial and should be drawn up professionally.

Tax considerations and ownership options

Which ownership option is right for you? Unfortunately, there is no one-size-fits-all answer. It will depend on your individual situation.

While we will have a look at some general rules below, it is recommended you get advice from a professional, like your accountant or lawyer, before you purchase a property, especially if you are buying in a syndicate.

If you are considering becoming a property investor and you do not have an accountant and a lawyer, engage both — now. Qualified accountants know the intricate tax rules, and lawyers understand the legalities, of property ownership. Good advisers — accountants and lawyers — who charge you a few hundred dollars a year will pay for themselves in multiples of that figure.

With that recommendation, there are still some rules of thumb to keep in mind in terms of how your property asset should be held. In general terms it is better to:

▲ have positively geared properties in the name of the lower income earner

▲ have negatively geared properties in the name of the higher income earner

▲ buy in joint names if you are on similar incomes.

Let's look at these rules a little more closely.

Positively geared properties in the name of a lower income earner

For this example, let's assume that we have a partnership that includes one partner who earns no income. The other is relatively highly paid, earning $110000 a year. The property being purchased is positively geared and will produce $5000 net income a year.

Because the property is in the name of the partner with no other income, he or she would now have an income of $5000, which is still below the tax-free threshold.

Using the 2006–2007 income tax rates, the working partner would be on a marginal tax rate of 41.5 per cent (including the Medicare levy). Because the $5000 is net income and if the property was in the name of the spouse earning $110 000, the 41.5 per cent tax rate would apply to the $5000. Tax of $2075 would be paid, leaving net income of $2925 (compare this with $5000 net income of the non-working spouse).

Negatively geared properties in the name of the higher income earner

With negative gearing it is arguably even more important to put the property under the name that provides the best tax benefits. The property is already causing you to 'lose' money, so compounding it with a poor ownership structure would only make things worse.

We'll assume the property is negatively geared and is showing an annual loss of $6000.

If the house was in the name of a non-earning partner, none of the $6000 could be reclaimed against tax, as the partner isn't paying any tax. That partner would effectively have an income of –$6000 for the year.

If the property was in the name of the higher earning partner, then he or she could claim back 41.5 per cent (the tax rate for those earning between $75 000 and $150 000 a year) or 46.5 per cent (the tax rate for people earning more than $150 000 a year) of those losses.

Taking the two extreme examples (a partner earning $0 a year and a partner earning more than $150 000 a year), the difference between having the negatively geared asset owned by the higher earning partner and the lower earning partner would be $3210 a year or more than $60 a week.

Buying in joint names if on similar incomes

Clearly if both partners are on similar incomes, or the purchase is being made by a syndicate, there will be few or no tax advantages in the property being held in one name.

Often, couples in their thirties and forties can be on similar incomes (particularly before children are brought into the equation) or, more generally, on the same marginal tax rate. If this is likely to be the case for an extended period, then it could be wise to hold the property in both names.

However, if there is a likelihood that one partner is going to take a cut in income in the next five years or so (for example, to have children, work part-time or study), it might make sense to put the investment property in the name of the partner who is likely to have the higher long-term income, because it will lead to a larger tax return.

Whatever the type of ownership structure you eventually choose, it's also important to take a long-term view before you lock yourself in. Just as the old investment adage says that you should never choose an investment based on tax minimisation alone, you should also never base your property investment decision solely on whose name you may put the title under.

Caution needs to be taken and advice sought from a lawyer about the ownership arrangements if it is not simply a traditional joint ownership. The name on the title can have a major impact in the future — including property disposals or asset splitting in the case of divorce, separation or a division within the family or group. Group purchases or syndicates, in particular, need exact advice on how to divide ownership in a way that will take into account each person's contributions.

Chapter 5

Where and what to buy

In this chapter we will cover the following:

▲   Picking a location

▲   Inner-city locations

▲   Suburban locations

▲   New housing estates

▲   Off the plan

▲   Rural and regional locations

▲   Areas on the way up

▲   Types of property

▲   Online search tools.

Picking a location

Most people buy a home within 7 kilometres of where they live or have previously lived. Sometimes the home is even close to where they grew up. This goes for investment purchases too.

Therefore, if you were to draw on a map a 7-kilometre circle around where you live now — whether you are a home owner, tenant or would-be property investor — the chances are you would buy a property within this area. One of the reasons for this is the 'familiarity factor'. People feel more comfortable buying in an area they know well — familiarity translates to increased confidence. The line of thinking behind this is, 'I already know most of the streets and locations, so I can reduce the risk compared with buying in an area I don't know'.

It's a bit territorial, a bit tribal and a bit self fulfilling. How many people have you met who have said they hate the area or suburb they live in? It's unlikely you know many — otherwise they wouldn't still be living there.

However, there is more to picking a location than just choosing an area you are familiar with — especially when you consider that location is probably one of *the* most important factors in your property investment decision.

Picking an investment property because it is just around the corner is usually a bad idea. For a start there is no diversification and if a major market change occurs in the area, both your home and your investment property could suffer. Real estate is like any other investment — it's not a good idea to have all your eggs in one basket.

Choose the wrong location and no matter how good the property is or how much you try to renovate or improve it, you will always be in that bad area.

Yes, some areas have been gentrified — many older inner suburbs previously overlooked by buyers are now trendy, upmarket locations. In most cases these areas have been improving for several decades — long enough for clever investors to know that these areas are not actually bad locations but locations that are on the 'way up'. (There is more on how to pick a location on the way up later in this chapter.)

Let's look at a couple of things that can make a location less appealing — or at least put you on alert and make you think twice before buying.

To most investors a bad location is simply one that has a chronic vacancy rate and an oversupply of properties to rent. It doesn't matter where it is — in the city, in the outer suburbs or in regional areas — if there is a history of high vacancies and short-term tenants, there is something wrong. Vacancy statistics are often available through the REIA and its affiliated state offices. Knowing the statistics will help you highlight black spots of high vacancies in your area.

In the current property cycle, most cities are experiencing strong rental demand and vacancies at historic lows. The traditional balance between supply and demand (the number of properties for rent and the number of tenants who want a place to rent) is generally reached when the market has a vacancy rate of about 3 per cent.

On average, vacancies higher than 3 per cent indicate that tenants have an advantage over landlords (because supply is outstripping demand), whereas vacancies below 3 per cent indicate that landlords have the upper hand (because demand is outstripping supply).

High vacancies can hurt property investors on two fronts. First, there is the obvious problem of attracting tenants. With all those other empty properties to choose from, tenants might want you to drop the rent or, worse, they might choose somewhere else to live and you won't get any rent!

Second, high vacancies can hurt property investors when it comes to sell. Owner-occupiers will be your main buyer group, which means you have a smaller potential pool of purchasers, less competition and, more than likely, a lower eventual sale price. That's why savvy investors steer clear of areas with chronic vacancy problems. If canny investors have done their homework on a location and found high vacancies, they will automatically discount any potential purchase price or not bother buying there at all.

So check with local agents, and keep an eye on websites and classified ads to see how long properties take to become tenanted in the area you are considering. Make friends with a few management agents and ask them what vacancy rates are like.

One of the hardest things to pinpoint is the reason why some areas just don't work well — and it's not always worth your time to try to find out. It can be because local industry is in a slump and jobs have been lost, or there might be severe noise, a lack of public transport or cultural issues. In fact, even fashion can make a suburb or region unpopular.

If you are a low-risk taker, assess the evidence at face value and look elsewhere, or buy at a big discount so you are less stressed about the risk of buying in such an area. If you are willing to take a punt, do a bit more research and see if you can work out what the problem is. One of the best ways to do this is by tapping into 'local knowledge' — and it usually means being a bit pushy!

Knock on the front door of homes near the property and introduce yourself to the occupants. Say that you are thinking of buying in the street and wondered what they thought of the area. How long have they been there? Why did they choose this area? Go to the local milk bar and talk to the people behind the counter (make sure you buy something as well). You will be surprised at how often people come out with interesting comments when they are asked for their opinion — everyone loves being asked what they think.

If you can establish the reason why the area is struggling, add it to your property equation. Can the problem be overcome? Once you know what it is, you can decide if it is worth the risk. If not, move on.

Oversupply

An oversupply of the same type of housing should also sound alarm bells when you are researching your location. In recent years this has been particularly obvious in high-density inner-city markets where there has been significant high-rise apartment development. In most of these locations — and almost every city in Australia has an area that can be classified in this group — the problem is not necessarily long lasting. Eventually, demand for these types of properties slows down and so does the construction. However, you don't want to sit around for years waiting for the capital value to increase, while tenants pick and choose their properties and, often, their rents (which will put downward pressure on all other rents nearby).

Also, if there are too many similar properties in the one area, often you will be forced to accept the rent level of the most financially stressed landlord. In other words, if Joe Blow is really squeezed to find a tenant, he might be willing to charge $100 a week for his one-bedroom apartment simply because he needs some income. You, on the other hand, are not under the same financial squeeze. But because Joe has rented out his apartment at $100, other would-be tenants will now also expect to pay only $100 for similar one-bedroom apartments. Whether he meant to or not, Joe Blow has put downward pressure on the area's market rents.

Inner-city locations

Inner-city living is high-density living; whether you are in a freestanding house or an apartment, you will be close to your neighbours. However, the benefits of inner-city living, such as cheap transport, lots of services, shops, entertainment and job opportunities, usually outweigh the negative aspects of living in high-density locations.

This means tenants and future property buyers are often willing to pay more for a property. Instead of buying a $50-a-week train pass to get to work from an outer suburb, the proximity of commercial centres to inner-city locations means you can walk to work or spend less time and money on public transport and travel. The convenience of having a choice of restaurants, night-life venues and shopping strips is also a much sought-after benefit of inner-city locations for which most people will pay more.

Landlords and property vendors can benefit from inner-city locations through higher rents, a larger pool of tenants and eventually higher resale prices. Instead of $50 spent on the train pass, it could mean a tenant can spend $50 more a week on rent — that means more in the landlord's pocket. A potential owner-occupier, on the other hand, might pay a higher price for an inner-city property because he or she can afford an extra $50 a week on the mortgage repayments, instead of the train pass.

The gentrification of many inner-city suburbs has seen astounding price growth during the past few decades. It would be true for most cities that the closer the area is to the central business district, the higher its price growth. So if you are looking for strong capital gains, the inner-city suburbs are a good bet.

Due to the strong capital gains (and high purchase prices) in inner-city suburbs, investors in this market are willing to accept that their annual rental income may not come close to covering the costs of the investment.

The downside of inner-city life is the constant congestion — on the roads, in the streets and in the few parkland areas available.

Traffic pollution is a factor for some people, while no room for a pet is another valid criticism from others. Although there are lots of reasons to live in the inner city, it's not for everyone.

While you will often attract young tenants to an inner-city area, frequently the buyers of these properties are baby boomers looking for city-side living to complement their country retreat. Remember to always keep your resale market in mind when you buy an investment property.

Suburban locations

In planning and demographic terms, metropolitan areas are often divided into rings, which radiate out from the central business district. Figure 5.1 (overleaf) shows the metropolitan rings and how they spread out from the central business district.

The middle ring

The middle-ring suburbs are usually between 7 kilometres and 15 kilometres from the CBD. (However, you should make your own assessment of your city or town.) If there is a physical barrier, such as a river or a range of hills, then usually this will create the 'ring' rather than a measure of distance. The middle-ring suburbs are often well-established areas with larger pieces of land (compared with the inner city), larger properties and often more parks and schools. It's basic Australian suburbia.

Often, houses within the middle ring are the most consistently priced type of property, having usually been built in development waves as the city has gradually expanded. Far from being on the outskirts as at the time they were built, they are now in the centre of most activity and services. The pace of development has usually been a bit more controlled compared with early inner-city development, when housing and industry were often competing for space.

Figure 5.1: the metropolitan rings in relation to the central business district

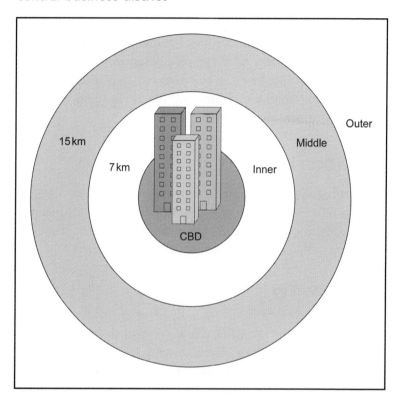

Middle-ring suburbs now have the added advantage of still being reasonably close to the city but out of the constant noise and bustle of the higher density inner-city suburbs.

As a general rule of thumb, middle-ring suburbs are those areas where the returns from purchase price and rental income are fairly well matched. (In comparison, the relatively high-priced inner-city market has an unbalanced purchase price to rental-income return situation.)

As the return ratio for purchase price and rental income is more-or-less equal in middle-ring suburbs, investors expect equal returns from a combination of the income and the eventual capital gain (generated from reselling the property at a new purchase price). These areas are also the traditional home of the family. Three- or four-bedroom houses in the middle rings should have a steady flow of would-be tenants and buyers.

The outer ring

Outer-ring suburbs, on the other hand, often have relatively low purchase prices but higher rents. This helps compensate the investor for slower capital gains.

The outer ring is the buffer between the new housing estates and the middle-ring suburbs. They often suffer from a bit of a no-man's-land complex for several years once the new estates start going up around them.

Houses in these outer-ring suburbs need to have an 'X' factor — something special that sets a property apart — to be worth purchasing, because otherwise the houses tend to be lumped into one big pot of 'sameness'.

On a larger scale, an X factor could be a themed suburb, such as a bushy area where subdivisions have been kept to large block sizes. This will give a suburb an edge over a rival area for some buyers or tenants.

Outer-ring houses can suffer from slow price growth as new housing estates nearby attract most of the new buyers, leaving the existing houses — often with little architectural or fashion merit — to languish.

New housing estates

New housing estates are typically on the outer fringes of the metropolitan area. Traditionally, they had poor public transport connections and a shortage of services such as schools and shops.

The housing estates of 10 or even five years ago, however, are nothing like the new estates.

Once seen as areas where young mothers were confined to the isolation and poverty of 'nappy-ville', as they were commonly called, the housing estates of today are more like totally planned communities. They often come complete with tree-lined streets and cutting-edge landscaping, ready-built schools and childcare, established shopping centres, and a host of recreational and support networks.

There are still drawbacks, however, and public transport is often the biggest. If there is a public transport connection, usually the timetable is limited and the cost prohibitive, simply because of the sheer distance from the city. These are factors that need to be weighed up when deciding on the location in which to buy an investment property.

But there are rewards for investors who target these markets. Most tenancy demand in a new estate will be from would-be owners in the area. Often, families or young couples will rent while their 'dream home' is under construction on the same estate or in one nearby.

Because there are relatively few properties for rent — most of the houses in new estates are already purchased and being built for owners to occupy — you may be able to name your price. The lack of rental properties means there is a scarcity of options for people who want to rent, which usually translates to higher rental income for the investor.

Rental income is likely to provide the major part of your total return from an investment in a housing estate, so try to ensure a reasonable return from your tenant each week or month rather than relying on future capital gain, which could lag behind the rest of the property market.

Traditionally, house price growth in new estates has been one of the slowest compared with other established housing markets — although the oversupply of inner-city apartments may be a close rival. This is because there is virtually an unending supply of new houses being built and they are often being built exactly to the requirements of their purchasers. So, naturally, there would be limited demand for an existing house, especially one that can't be tailor-made.

But there is always an upside. As an investor without any emotional bias towards a particular property, you will be able to drive a hard bargain on any homes that come up for resale, and your purchase price is likely to be substantially less than that of a similar home in an older or more established area.

Off the plan

Buying off the plan means buying a property that isn't built yet. You literally choose and buy from a plan, rather than walking around and inspecting an actual property.

Often, the only things you have to inform your decision are a small-scale model of the development, a set of floor plans and a showroom with materials, finishes, and examples of colour schemes. When you are buying off the plan you are putting a lot of faith in the developer. You must trust that you will get what you think you are buying because you are committing yourself to a purchase contract and usually paying a deposit before you ever see the real thing.

There are benefits and drawbacks in buying off the plan and only you will know if any pre-construction savings are worth the risk of buying something unseen.

The benefits of buying property off the plan are mostly cost savings. In some states you won't have to pay as much stamp duty when you buy off the plan. Because the property is not yet built, the stamp duty is calculated on the value of the property at the time of purchase. For example, if the property is still just an empty site with a few footings poured, then your portion of the development is extremely low, which means the stamp duty will be very low.

The drawbacks, or risks, of buying property off the plan are many. The biggest risk is that you will not be happy with the finished product.

The best way to reduce this risk is to carefully scrutinise the details of what you are buying. Make sure every detail and promise is in writing—including basic construction issues such as building materials, ceiling heights and window sizes. It's important to remember that, often, display properties have added features that aren't included in the basic plan. There are many stories of people who bought off the plan thinking they were buying the exact replica of the showroom or display apartment, only to find that the display apartment's 13-foot ceilings were actually only standard 8-foot ceilings on the plan.

Handy hint

Some of the items you should be sure about before agreeing to an off-the-plan contract include the following:

- total land/area size
- external building materials
- internal building materials
- ceiling heights
- window sizes
- light fittings
- number and location of power outlets
- floor coverings
- internal paintwork (including how many coats on walls, woodwork, etc.)
- glass thickness
- insulation (sound and heat)
- exact room sizes
- door widths
- balcony/terrace sizes
- appliances
- bathroom fittings (by item number)
- window coverings.

The contract

An experienced property lawyer will be your best bet for making sure all your expectations of design features and materials are covered. However, just as important, a lawyer will also ensure that clauses relating to what happens when your expectations aren't met are included in the contract.

The contract must also include a remedy that you can live with. You may also want to include a time penalty in the agreement. If the development takes much longer than expected, you may have to find alternative accommodation, delay the sale of another property or delay other decisions, or forgo rental income. It's worth remembering that you might be suspended in financial limbo if there is a required minimum period of time before you can take legal redress.

Rural and regional locations

Country and coastal property markets have been undergoing a resurgence in the past five years, boosted by sea-changers and tree-changers shifting down a gear and heading off for the 'good life'.

From the number of television shows about the sea-change lifestyle, you could be forgiven for thinking that all of Australia is undergoing a regional property resurgence. However, in reality, only select areas are benefiting from the demographic shift.

Coastal towns are taking the biggest slice of the sea-change cake with population growth in coastal areas running at almost double the rest of Australia.

Population growth in regional areas within a half-day's drive to a city is also on the rise; and towns within two or three hours' drive of the city are benefiting even more from both permanent sea-changers and the surging holiday-home market.

This increased demand should be seen as a high-frequency alert to property investors, because increased demand means higher rents and higher capital gains.

However, there has already been significant price growth within a lot of non-metropolitan areas — particularly coastal townships along the eastern seaboard during the past few years. In some locations the growth will now be starting to slow down. But, fortunately, even if the sea-change shift starts to taper in the near future, there is another even more powerful demographic group rapidly bringing up the rear.

Baby boomers

Baby boomers — possibly the largest, richest and healthiest ageing population group ever documented in Australia — are searching for potential retirement homes in these same coastal and regional locations ahead of their eventual retirement in the next decade or less.

Many of them are looking to secure a property while they think prices are still reasonable, so they can use it as a part-time holiday home or weekender before moving in full-time. They are also taking long-term rentals on properties, so they can 'test the water' before making a financial commitment.

This powerful group also has plenty of money to spend and they will undoubtedly demand higher levels of service, shops and social facilities than most sleepy towns provide. This should also be a light-bulb moment for investors, as many of these areas will undergo significant redevelopment to meet demand for both housing and retail services.

But the key issue to keep in mind with these regional areas is that they will usually offer a higher risk than their city cousins. The main reason for this is that the population, and therefore the number of potential tenants and purchasers, is limited in rural and coastal areas. Another reason is that land in country (although not coastal) areas is not a scarce commodity. In fact, it's probably pretty cheap and plentiful, with supply outstripping demand.

Areas on the way up

Almost everyone knows somebody who bought into a suburb at the bottom of the market and has since sat back and watched it boom. During the past 20 years, almost every Australian city has seen its inner suburbs revitalised.

Handy hint

Unlike the popular real estate rule, 'always buy the worst house in the best street', picking an area on the way up is not a case of buying in the worst suburb in the best city.

Former working-class slums and abandoned middle-class homes have been renovated and revitalised in order to look like they did in their former glory days — or, in the case of most of the working-class areas, these homes have even reached new highs. Suddenly, even the shabbiest single-fronted worker's cottage, or darkest, dampest semi-detached inner-city home has taken on luxuries never imagined by the builders of those humble late 19th and early 20th century properties.

Let's think about where the next areas on the way up will be. There are certain indicators that will tell you when areas are on the way up.

Things to look for include:

▲ an increase in number of homes being renovated (indicates people have money and are prepared to invest in the suburb)

▲ an increase in retail and commercial properties being renovated (shows that business people also think it's worth sticking around and investing money in the area)

▲ a change in social or cultural mix of the area (for example, older people selling up or younger people moving in)

▲ an increase in household earnings — because higher household incomes indicate an improving socio-economic situation (these statistics can be seen in the census data, or the local council may also provide you with this information)

▲ a high number of cafes and fashion stores (indicates an affluent and trendy suburb)

▲ community issues and local news stories that give you an insight into the economic state of an area and the attitude and aspirations of its residents (read the local newspaper)

▲ relatively highly developed areas (few vacant sites or empty land blocks usually indicate a scarcity of land that, in turn, means higher prices for existing properties)

▲ streets and areas with a particular architectural style (period-style homes, be they Inter-war, Californian bungalow, Victorian, 1960s hip, Art Deco or Edwardian, all have a rarity value worth considering)

▲ the features of neighbouring suburbs (if the area you have targeted is surrounded by 'good' suburbs, the chances are those people and positive factors will start to spill into the adjoining area).

Types of property

In the following section we will take a look at various types of property in terms of their viabiliy as investments.

Houses

Freestanding houses, of all the property types, are probably the most versatile and dependable. As rental properties, they will appeal to a wide range of potential tenants, from share houses to families. As purchase options, the market is also pretty wide, appealing to both other investors and owner-occupiers. Maintenance costs, however, will be relatively high, especially if you have to keep up appearances with a garden. Weatherboard houses also have more maintenance issues than brick or concrete construction. However, on the plus side, rotten weatherboards are easily and more cheaply repaired compared with re-pointing or underpinning brickwork.

Three-bedroom properties traditionally have the most consistent rent increases and demand from tenants. However, the forces of supply and demand will always control the market.

Did you know?

Median rent increases of two- and three-bedroom houses during the year to March 2006 were as follows:

Capital city	Two-bedroom rent increases (%)	Three-bedroom rent increases (%)
Adelaide	+8.8	+6.8
Brisbane	+11.1	+6.3
Canberra	+7.1	+3.3
Darwin	+10.0	+11.1
Hobart	+15.9	+8.7
Melbourne	+4.5	+4.5
Perth	+29.4	+20.0
Sydney	+3.4	+1.9

Source: REAL ESTATE INSTITUTE OF AUSTRALIA

Semi-detached

These typically inner-city or middle-ring brick homes often have limited access to sunlight — especially if they are on the south side of another property. However, they are popular rental properties and, because they are more common in inner- to middle-ring suburbs, have a good record of capital gains.

Renovation techniques during the past decade have included adding second storeys to the rear of these homes, as well as creating new and bigger light wells to overcome the lack of sunlight. These properties usually have small rear and front yards and limited (if any) off-street parking. You should check with the adjoining property's owner to see if he or she has any redevelopment or renovation plans.

Townhouses

Typically, two-storey modern developments and townhouses are considered a step up from apartment and unit blocks. They usually have a land component, but this can be quite limited and in some developments may be included as common land and not on the property's title.

Townhouses are generally two- to four-bedroom properties, depending on the development. In most cases they are run by a body corporate and are strata titled. They are popular with younger tenants and are usually in reasonably high-density areas. The contemporary design of most townhouses means they appeal to a wide range of tenants. However, stairs in two-storey properties are often avoided by young families and older people.

....

Did you know?

Median rent increases for apartments and townhouses (other dwellings) during the year to March 2006 were as follows:

Adelaide	+8.8%	Hobart	+15.9%
Brisbane	+11.1%	Melbourne	+4.5%
Canberra	+7.1%	Perth	+29.4%
Darwin	+10.0%	Sydney	+3.4%

Source: REAL ESTATE INSTITUTE OF AUSTRALIA

Apartments

Apartments and units come in almost every configuration and can comprise of every construction material you can think of. Be they high-rise, tilt-slab concrete or low-rise, six-pack, walk-up brick flats — apartments have traditionally been the first investment step for many people and also the first rental property for many new tenants.

In almost every development cycle there has been concern about oversupply of apartments. In the 1920s, when apartment living became prevalent, people criticised the influx of cheaper housing. Art Deco apartments, once shunned as housing for the less well off, are now highly sought after. The typical 1960s brick blocks built in little squares all around the country were also snubbed, while the introduction of cheap and fast construction materials (such as blue board and tilt slab) and a lack of soundproofing in some of today's projects have been cause for criticism.

Despite the detractors, apartments are still a very popular investment choice. They offer a relatively cheap entry point into property ownership and they are usually relatively low maintenance.

Two-bedroom apartments are probably the most versatile in terms of choice of tenant and the cost of purchase. Two-bedroom apartments can easily rent to two friends, a couple who also want a spare room or home office, a couple and their friend, a small family of mum and dad (or sole parent) and a child, or, of course, a single person.

Also, the cost of construction of a two-bedroom apartment is not double the cost of building a one-bedroom apartment, so the purchase price is usually cheaper than a one-bedroom property on a per-square-metre basis.

One-bedroom apartments with study areas or a sunroom are also popular purchases. The study area—while not necessarily completely separate—allows for a sofa bed, play area, TV room or office desk for extra flexibility.

Did you know?

Houses versus apartments—price growth (year to March 2006) is as follows:

Capital city	Houses (% growth)	Other dwellings (apartments, etc.) (% growth)
Adelaide	+0.7	−4.9
Brisbane	+3.0	+7.5
Canberra	+2.5	+3.3
Darwin	+21.8	+33.3
Hobart	+4.2	−0.5
Melbourne	+4.2	+5.3
Perth	+23.9	+22.2
Sydney	−3.6	−3.0

Source: REAL ESTATE INSTITUTE OF AUSTRALIA

Larger apartments are also being sought by baby boomers or empty nesters as 'city' homes. There is an increasing trend where older Australians are selling off the large family home and buying two alternative and smaller properties. Often, this involves an apartment — albeit a bit more upmarket than the average apartment — and a coastal or rural home.

Online search tools

Hopefully, we have given you a rough idea about finding the right location and type of property. Now it's time to start searching.

Newspapers have comprehensive lists of, and advertising for, properties for sale in your city or local area. They are also a ready source of dates and times for auctions and open for inspections. Newspapers are great for carrying around with you as you search for your perfect property.

However, while newspapers are a handy search tool, the easiest and most efficient way to find a property is to use the internet.

Online searching is easy and quick — just log on to the website and follow the hints. This method of property research involves typing in the area you want and looking at what's available. You can quickly narrow down your search by also including the property type or the price range you are interested in.

As well as looking for properties to buy, the web is also a useful tool for checking out areas with which you are not familiar, and for finding information on an interstate or overseas property. While you are at it, also check out the properties for rent. This will give you an idea of potential returns in the areas you are considering.

....

Tried and true

Michelle has bought her last three properties over the internet using <realestate.com.au>. The only time Michelle

Tried and true *(cont'd)*

physically saw the properties was on the days she signed the purchase contracts.

In each case she had been looking at interstate markets and had narrowed down the search to three potential properties. For the last purchase she flew to Brisbane and inspected all three (they all stacked up to her list of requirements) before signing up for one of them that day.

Choose a couple of properties to actually go and have a look at — whether you are buying or trying to gauge how much rent you can expect. Although you can pretty much narrow down the search through the internet and the newspaper, you should still go and have a look for yourself — there are some things that you will need to see for yourself.

Checklist for researching your investment property

☑ *Scarcity value*: Any property — whether it's an apartment, house or warehouse conversion — with a scarcity value should hold its value. A property being one of a kind, because of an oddity, is not necessarily such a good thing because it can limit your market for tenants and buyers. But a property that can't be reproduced, because it's from a certain architectural period or is in an area where there will be no more development, will usually have ongoing demand.

☑ *Location:* Check out the street, the neighbourhood and the whole suburb. Walk around the property and look at the next-door properties. Are there overlooking windows? What type of people live in the area? What services and public transport does the suburb have? Talk to the milkbar owner and speak to the neighbours. Is there a lot of new development or are most of the houses already established?

☑ *Type of property:* Ask yourself about the type of tenants that will suit the property. For example, if it is a three-bedroom home, your greatest pool of potential tenants will be a family or share house. Which type of tenants do you want? Ask yourself who will buy this property from you when it comes time to sell. The biggest buyer group will give you the best competition and best price. If you are considering buying an apartment, make sure you ask the seller for a copy of the body corporate rules so you know what you are getting into. Also, see if you can find out who the other tenants or owners in the apartment block are.

Chapter 6

Setting your price and negotiating with the agent

In this chapter we will cover the following:

▲   How much should you pay?

▲   Valuing a property

▲   Evaluating special features

▲   Rental guarantees

▲   Negotiating with the agent

▲   Auctions

▲   Private sales

▲   Tenders

▲   When to walk away.

How much should you pay?

Aside from location, price is the most important issue when it comes to buying property. In fact, sometimes a property's price can be more important than its location!

There is a saying within clever property circles that is good to keep in mind when buying a property: 'You make your profit when you make your purchase.' The saying basically means that you should 'buy well'. If you can get your head around this concept, then you are less likely to pay the wrong price.

A good starting point for 'buying well' is to make sure your purchase price is within your budget and within the market price for the type of house and location you have chosen. Of course, it is even better if the price is below your budget and below the market price, as that way you make your profit from day one.

As a quick guide to see if you're on the right track with the price you are planning to pay, ask yourself this question: 'If I had to quickly sell this property, say in six months' time, would I get my money back?' If the answer is yes, then you are unlikely to be paying too much. If the answer is no, then your offer price might be too high. To help you answer this question, find out how long properties are taking to sell in the area.

Making your profit when you make your purchase, however, also requires you to know the locations and prices of other properties in your market segment. It is only after you have this 'market intelligence' that you can properly judge if your price is below or above the market rate.

To gain greater market intelligence there are additional questions you can ask yourself that will guide your thinking before going ahead with your offer price. They include:

▲   Do you expect to recoup your buying costs (purchase price, stamp duty, mortgage costs and other extra costs at the time of buying) if you have to sell within six months?

▲ Do you also expect to recoup your selling costs (such as the agent's commission and advertising fees) if you have to sell within six months?

▲ Will you have to spend money on the property to sell it and break even?

▲ Will you have a ready market of buyers who will want to buy this property?

▲ If there are no buyers, will there be tenants willing to pay the rent you need to earn so you can keep the property?

The answers will help you decide if you are paying the right price.

Valuing a property

It can be argued that the ultimate value of a property is the price someone is prepared to pay. In other words, if someone is willing to spend $320000 on a two-bedroom apartment, then that is its value.

But this is not always so — the property's sale or purchase price can be quite different to its value. People buy under the value and they buy over the value. Your aim should always be to buy under the property's real value.

Valuing property has a whole profession built around it. It is a difficult and important expertise that you, as a property investor, are going to have to master to avoid paying too much, or worse, missing a golden opportunity.

There are various methods for valuing a property. They usually involve calculations based on:

▲ land size

▲ building size

▲ location

- ▲ construction materials
- ▲ income-earning ability
- ▲ best and highest use
- ▲ economic conditions
- ▲ resale market.

One of the most common ways to get a rough idea of value is to compare a property with similar properties. A three-bedroom house in a middle-ring suburb in a quiet street with off-street parking is going to be valued at roughly the same price as an identical three-bedroom house with off-street parking in the same area. The drawback with this valuation method, however, is that you really need as many examples as possible. Just comparing one sale price will put you at risk of overpaying if that house achieved a price higher than its underlying value. If possible, collect the sale prices of the past six months for the area you are considering. Then compare the building and land size and also the construction type. This should give you a good idea of what the going rate is.

Replacement construction value and replacement purchase value

A more technical way to assess a property's value is to use a combination of methods.

Most builders and real estate agents (or valuers) can give you a rough guide as to the capital cost per square metre of the type of property you are considering. The builder will be able to give you a fairly accurate estimate of how much it will cost to build a similar property (known as the replacement construction value) while a real estate agent will be able to supply you with a price per square metre that other properties in the area have sold for (the replacement purchase value).

Armed with these two estimates — the replacement construction value and the replacement purchase value — you are less likely to go wrong with your estimated value of a property.

Best and highest use

'Best and highest use' is a term used by valuers to look at the potential that a property has. It is usually applied to commercial properties; however, it also has its place in residential markets.

A derelict house that is in a good location and on a big block of land is going to have a 'best and highest use' value that is much greater than the sum of its land value and the value of the house itself. This is because there is the potential for a new development (such as a commercial centre or apartments) being built on the land, which could add to the property's value when it comes time to sell. Always keep in mind future development, rezoning or renovation when considering the best and highest use value of a property.

Evaluating special features

Less tangible features to consider when valuing your property include scarcity value, appearance, the cache of certain areas, proximity to schools and even neighbouring properties.

Scarcity

If the property up for sale is a two-storey townhouse in a development of 50 other identical townhouses, there is not likely to be any scarcity value. This should suggest to you, as an investor, that at almost any time there might be another townhouse just like this one that will come up for sale — so there is no need to go out of your way to purchase it.

However, if the townhouse is one of five in the middle of a highly prized suburb where the only other homes are large mansions, then a smaller home can earn a significant premium because it is scarce in this type of location. You could be justified, therefore, in paying at the top of your valuation range for this property; traditionally, smaller (and cheaper) houses in high-priced suburbs are in strong demand and usually hold and grow their value very well.

Land size

Land size — and the potential to redevelop or strata title — is a major component in the valuation process. If there are two similar three-bedroom houses, usually the one with the larger piece of land will have a higher value. This also goes for an apartment or townhouse that has a land component included on its title, as compared with one that doesn't have any land.

The neighbourhood

The neighbourhood, too, has an impact on a property's value. Take the example of two similar three-bedroom houses again, but, this time, imagine that one is next to a shopping strip and the other is two streets back from the shops. A shopping strip location is less desirable for some buyers because of high vehicle traffic, noise levels, early morning commercial cleaners, high pedestrian numbers and possible parking problems — even if it has a slightly greater land size.

However, if you look at the situation from a different angle, there could be some hidden value in this property for you. If the shopping strip is successful there may be opportunity to expand. This could mean the three-bedroom house next to the shopping strip actually has the potential to be redeveloped for retail or commercial use — lifting its higher and better use value — which usually means higher value overall.

Unique features

A unique or unusual property, too, has its pluses and minuses. A rare property often has a premium attached to it, but not always.

It can be very difficult to assess the value of one-off properties, such as a unique warehouse conversion, a historic home or a penthouse apartment. It will be harder to judge the value of these types of property against others because there will be nothing to compare them with — even the replacement construction value may not be an accurate guide. In this case, possibly the biggest issue to think about, in terms of value, is your potential resale market. Even though you haven't bought the property yet, you still have to think about the endgame — the sale.

Take another look at this one-off property and decide if you are likely to have a ready market of buyers when the time comes to sell. Sometimes one-off properties can be so rare that many people may not want to take a risk buying or renting them. Regardless of the price, it may mean you will have to wait longer to sell or rent them.

Luxurious features

Features that are considered luxurious, such as swimming pools, saunas, gymnasiums and tennis courts, can also either add or subtract value from a property. Buyers often see these features as negatives for the following reasons:

▲ Many older families no longer want a backyard that is taken up with a swimming pool and would prefer it to be filled in.

▲ Saunas may sound good to people who use them regularly but they will likely be a drawback for someone who doesn't want the extra cost or maintenance around their home.

▲ Gymnasiums built in the garage or in basement areas may not be highly valued by many buyers — or tenants — unless they also happen to be like-minded about exercise. If the room or area can't be used for any other purpose then it will often be discounted from the valuation process.

▲ Tennis courts mean more land, which usually spells a higher valuation. However, even tennis courts can be a headache for those owners who don't have the funds to pay for the upkeep or who never use them. Selling off the tennis court is also only going to be possible if there is separate access to the land and subdivision approval is possible.

Rental guarantees

Rental guarantees are increasingly common these days with many new residential projects being sold with the promise of a certain level of income each year. Rental guarantees, however, can be misleading and give you a false sense of security. The value, or cost, of a rental guarantee is often built into the upfront purchase price — which means you are paying for it.

Developers and some property managers, such as serviced apartment operators, usually offer rental guarantees based on a percentage of your purchase price. This is a sales technique to help reduce your pre-purchase nerves. It is meant to demonstrate that the developer or manager is confident that a project will have strong demand and earn a good return. However, regardless of what the rental guarantee is, it may or may not have any bearing on the real rent.

If a property is being marketed with a 7 per cent rental guarantee, then that 7 per cent may be topped up by the developer or the manager. It may never be a realistic rental and it is certainly not something you can rely on or expect to achieve once your property goes on the open market and is at the mercy of market forces.

How a rental guarantee can be built into your purchase price

If you buy a $500000 investment property with a 6 per cent rental guarantee, you would expect to receive $30000 a year in rental income.

This rent will come from the organisation that has given you the guarantee—either the developer, a third-party financier or a manager or operator. Unbeknown to you, the manager or developer may only be receiving $25000 from a tenant each year and he or she will be topping it up by $5000 to meet the requirements of the guarantee.

This is a calculated move. The developer may estimate that he or she will have to top up each property by $5000 a year for the life of the guarantee, which can be from one year to three years, depending on the sales pitch. That means the developer will have to spend $15000 over three years to meet the rental guarantee on your property. But in reality this $15000 has often already been factored in to the sale price. The chances are your property was originally valued at only $485000 before the guarantee was put in place.

In some cases, you can discount the price by buying without the guarantee—but, obviously, that means you are on your own in terms of what level of income you will earn. If you do decide to buy without the guarantee, you should get independent advice on rental levels in the area.

Guarantees do give some buyers peace of mind. They can be a bit like fixed-interest rates on a mortgage. A guarantee will let you know exactly what your income is going to be and you will not have to worry about market forces or periods of vacancy during the term of the guarantee. In many ways it is like putting off the risk of your purchase for a few years until the guarantee runs out.

Who is offering the guarantee?

If you are buying a property with a rental guarantee, take a good hard look at who is guaranteeing the rent. Is it the developer? Is it a third-party financial institution? Is it a property manager?

Once you know the exact identity of this organisation or company, do a company search. This can be done on the Australian Securities & Investments Commission's (ASIC) website, <www.asic.gov.au>. Try to find out who owns the company and how long it has been in business. A guarantee is only as good as the company standing behind it — a fly-by-night company equals a fly-by-night guarantee.

Eventually the guarantee comes to an end and you are faced with the original risk. Perhaps you are thinking that the rental market will be stronger after the guarantee runs out, or that the property's capital value will have increased by then and you will be able to sell at a profit. Whatever you're thinking, one thing any valuer will warn you about is that you are buying the underlying property, not the rental guarantee.

In other words, you must be sure the property stacks up to all your purchase and investment criteria first — think of the guarantee as an extra consideration, as either a bonus or a potential discount, depending on whether you decide to buy with or without it. Don't ever purchase a property because the rental guarantee makes it seem good. Once the guarantee is over, you may never get that much rental income again.

Negotiating with the agent

You may not feel very powerful when it comes to negotiating with a real estate agent — but remember that you do have some power. After all, you hold the key to the sale — and the key is your money! An agent can't sell a property if there is no buyer.

However, regardless of what you and the agent discuss, the vendor doesn't have to sell. So, ultimately, the vendor has the greatest power in this three-way negotiating feat.

Playing negotiating games is a huge waste of time. If you just want to test the market and find out details about prices, or inspect other properties to inform your knowledge of the market, say that's what you are doing. There is no need to pretend anything other than what you are really doing.

If you are a first-time investor learning about property, don't try to come across as a seasoned buyer. You won't fool anyone but you may make a fool of yourself.

Agents can spot a fake from 100 paces and if you waste their time, the only impression you are likely to give is one of mistrust if, or when, you deal with them again in the future.

Instead, explain yourself truthfully and you may make a valuable contact. If agents know you are genuine and what type of property you are looking for, then they may contact you when one becomes available.

But ultimately, every negotiation boils down to an offer and acceptance. You are the only one able to decide what to offer and the vendor is the only one who can decide what to accept — everything else is toing and froing. Yes, you can explain the reasons why you are offering a price below what the agent has indicated, but they don't have to be taken into account by the agent or the seller.

Getting professional advice is one way to back up your reasons for discounting a price. A building inspection, pest report, soil test or an architect's opinion can help vendors in their ultimate decision. However, it is possible that the owner already knows these facts and is waiting for potential buyers who haven't done their homework.

Real estate agents must operate within the laws of each state — and the regulations are all slightly different — as well as within the codes of conduct of their professional organisations, such as the REIA. If you think an agent is not conducting business in a professional manner, contact the principal of the agency and speak to him or her about it. If you don't see any improvement, you can make a formal complaint to the professional organisation, your local consumer affairs office, fair trading department, or communicate your grievances directly to the property owner.

One thing likely to get an agency to sit up and take notice is someone going above their head direct to their client — the vendor. After all, real estate agents are intermediaries, or brokers, and they therefore rely on people placing a value on their service and expertise. If a vendor thinks the agent is not acting in his or her best interest, there is likely to be swift action.

However, vendors and real estate agents know that buyers also have their tactics, and contacting the owner directly when there is no need is one of them. If you do this you are unlikely to win any negotiating points and it will usually put you at risk of getting both the owner and the agent offside.

Understating your budget is another common buyer tactic. Of course, you do not have to disclose to anyone what your budget is; however, many agents will assume you can go that extra bit if necessary. If you are frequently being recommended properties that are truly out of your budget, say so — don't pretend you don't like the properties for other reasons.

There are plenty of tip sheets on trying to 'get one over' the agent or the seller, but most agents know these so-called tips inside out. In the end, negotiations come down to a willing buyer and a willing seller.

Give your best offer, be it at auction or private sale, and see what happens.

Above all, don't be pressured into buying something you are unsure about. If you have second thoughts about a purchase, stop the process and take time out to rethink.

Salespeople, particularly the highly methodical and practised sales reps at new apartment projects and developments, are trained at putting pressure on buyers. It is part of their selling technique and is perceived as being a way to 'crunch the deal'.

When negotiating with salespeople, there are a few indicators that should sound warning bells for you. These include being told:

▲ The price is for a limited time only.

▲ The agent can pressure the owner/boss into accepting the deal.

▲ The price is a special discount just for you.

▲ You don't have to pay anything now but that you should just sign the contract anyway.

▲ Anything that sounds too good to be true (if it sounds too good to be true, it usually is).

If you become caught in a high-pressure sales situation, you should keep these things in mind:

▲ Do not sign anything.

▲ Tell the salesperson you have to get advice.

▲ Tell the salesperson you do not understand the contract.

▲ Ask for all information/prices/promises/guarantees to be in writing.

Auctions

Auctions are a popular sales method in areas with strong demand, such as inner-city and metropolitan locations. Auctions are often held on-site, on the street in front of the property that is for sale or in the rooms of the auctioneer or real estate agent. If it is in the agent's rooms, there is usually a bulk lot offered in the one session, often up to 20 properties, with a picture of each house put up on a screen as they are auctioned. Whatever the location, auctions are often a fast way to buy or sell.

This selling technique builds up everybody's expectation of a sale — the buyers *and* the sellers — and the auction hurly-burly often carries people along in its momentum. Advocates of auctions say they are a good way to concentrate demand into a relatively short period of time.

Traditionally, four to six weeks are spent advertising the property and holding 'open for inspections' before the auction is conducted. During this time potential buyers are crammed into half-hour or one-hour open-for-inspection periods because it helps build an impression of high demand for that particular property. In some cases this makes buyers confident that they're looking at a popular property so that they may be willing to pay a little more than they first thought.

On the day of the auction, the auctioneer also does his or her best to create a bit of drama and urgency about the property, with the hope that it will result in a sale. The presence of buyer competition can also increase the size of bids from people who have a competitive streak. Even those who are less likely to be pushed beyond their budgets can see for themselves if there really are other buyers out there and to what price level they are prepared to go.

Bidding

Make sure the auctioneer can see you if you intend to bid. Ensure that your bids are clear and loud. Standing in front and looking towards the auction crowd—you can stand almost beside the auctioneer—enables you to see who is doing the bidding. However, because you are not within easy view of the auctioneer you will have to make your bids clear or risk being overlooked. This position also puts you in full view of the crowd, so it's not for retiring types.

Auctioneers recommend buyers bid strongly and quickly, which means bidding loudly and quickly following up any counterbid with a new one of your own. This strategy is meant to indicate to your rival bidders that you are very keen and will keep counterbidding. It may put some novice bidders off but it will never intimidate a seasoned bidder. Strong and fast bidding is also an advantage to the auctioneer because it moves the auction along at a fast pace, which is something they always strive for.

If a property does not sell at auction, the agents usually negotiate with the highest bidder. If a deal is not finalised, then other bidders might be approached to see if they are able to go any higher. If no sale eventuates, the property is either listed for sale or withdrawn, depending on what the vendor decides to do.

Private sales

Properties up for private sale can have an unlimited sales period, depending on the demand for the particular type of property, the vendor's urgency to sell, its location and, of course, its price. When owners decide to privately sell, they either hire an agent or do it themselves, and they usually start advertising the property with an asking price. This can take a matter of weeks or months depending on the demand.

Although in most cases the advertised price is not the final sale price, the offer closest to the asking price usually buys the property. However, as a buyer, you don't have to take any notice of this asking price — after all, it is usually what the vendor thinks the property is worth and, not unsurprisingly, vendors often overestimate the value of their property.

Regardless of the asking price, you need to start your own evaluation of the property from scratch. Only after you decide on its value can you decide what price to offer.

In most situations your price will be below the asking price, but don't let that stop you from putting in an offer — sometimes the vendors really don't know the market and are just testing to see what price might be possible. The worst that can happen is that you receive a 'no thanks, too low' response. If you know your market, you'll know if it is you or the vendor who is being unrealistic and you can make your next move based on that.

Just how many times you are prepared to make an offer and a counteroffer is totally up to you. However, bear in mind human nature — inching up your offer each time by $250 could irritate the owner and prompt him or her to ignore you all together.

Most agents will let you know if there is someone else interested in the property and will give you an opportunity to counter an offer; however, don't rely on this. If you want to buy the property, be up-front and say so; after all, you can only give it your best shot or walk away.

In rare cases you might decide the asking price is lower than your valuation. Do a final check on all your numbers and make an offer at the asking price or just under. In this situation there should be little reason for any further negotiations, unless the vendor suddenly decides that he or she, too, thinks the price is too low.

Tenders

Tenders are a popular method of selling commercial real estate; however, they are also used to sell large and unusual residential properties. Examples of residential properties that have been sold through tender might include an exclusive multimillion-dollar beach house, a large rural estate or a historic mansion.

When a property is listed for sale by tender, potential buyers are sometimes asked to lodge a small deposit and in return they receive a copy of the tender documents. These documents contain the relevant sales information, including the details of owners and tenants.

The deposit is a display of good faith and an attempt to reduce copious tender documents, which are often expensive to produce. It also helps prevent confidential information about the vendor or the property being too widely known.

Generally, a sale by tender is more private than other selling methods. The details of the property are only given to genuine buyers and the inspections are carried out on the same basis.

Tenders will have a date and a time for when they close — meaning that you will have to lodge your written and sealed offer before that deadline.

Normally, you only get one shot with a tender. Your tender must nominate the price and any terms you want to make and it must also include a bank cheque for the deposit.

The tenders are usually opened under the scrutiny of a third-party solicitor or auditor to ensure that they are recorded properly and that any late tenders haven't slipped in after the others have been opened and the contents known.

Ultimately, the decision is up to the vendor. Usually the tender with the highest offer wins the property, although a lower offer can win if it is more appealing in other ways. For example, a vendor might choose the tender with a lower price but a shorter settlement, or a lower price but no conditions (such as being subject to finance).

Some tenders can also conduct a second round, depending on the conditions of the original tender. In this case, a chosen few will be asked to resubmit offers; but, more typically, tenders are one-shot wonders. They try to create the same 'urgency' that auctions do by giving potential buyers a limited time to make a decision and put in an offer. Unlike auctions, however, tenders don't let you see or hear about the competition or even if there is anyone else bidding. Also, unlike private sales and auctions, you usually don't get a second chance, so your offer should always be your best price.

When to walk away

Property buyers often say they feel as if they are at a big disadvantage when negotiating with an agent. Well, you can be if you let it happen!

Real estate agents seem to have all the answers and they keep them close to their chests. They know — or have a good idea of — the vendor's lowest acceptable price. They usually also know all the ins and outs of an area, the prices of neighbouring properties, the best streets, the best aspects, the hidden drawbacks, the level of demand and the likely rental income for most properties.

However, don't forget that you, on the other hand, know your budget, a bit about the market and hopefully the neighbourhood. So while you are probably at a disadvantage compared with the agent, you still have considerable power.

Also, no matter how much toing and froing goes on during negotiations, you are free to walk away. The agent, on the other hand, has a primary duty to the vendor, so is not free to walk away from you.

If your best offer is not good enough to buy the property, look elsewhere. If there is no other competition, the agent will probably contact you again. If the property sells to someone else, the price was above your budget so you couldn't (and shouldn't) have bought it anyway.

At some stage in your investment search you will probably have to decide to walk away from a property. If you are doing your buying based on rational financial criteria, the decision should be easy. (Many people who can't help but include a bit of emotion in the decision find it difficult to leave.)

There is no place for emotion. Don't be competitive. Don't be drawn to increase your offer if you can't afford it. If your best offer is not enough — walk away.

Chapter 7

How to finance your property deal

In this chapter we will cover the following:

▲ Online tools — the internet revolution

▲ Assessing your borrowing risk

▲ Mortgage brokers

▲ Becoming a valued bank client

▲ Interest rates — the unknown factor

▲ Fixed interest rates

▲ Preparing a business plan

▲ Documents the bank will want to see.

Unlike your home — which is about having a place for you to live — property investment is all about making money. And as most investment property is bought using borrowed money — loans that could go on for a decade or two — it's important to get the financing of your investment right from the start.

A loan for your first investment property could provide you with the biggest debt you have ever taken on, particularly if you haven't bought a home in recent years. In fact, depending on how long it has been since you last took out a property loan, you may find that a lot has changed over the years.

Borrowing for your first investment property could see you doubling, or tripling, the amount of debt you currently hold. If, in future years, you go on to buy several more properties, you may find yourself more than $1 million in debt. Ensuring that you properly structure the financing of your investment property will play a major part in making your investment a success.

Plus, property investment loans open doors that you might not have been aware existed before. Like all businesses, banks look after their bigger customers—and because property investors often carry a lot of debt, banks tend to do special deals for them. Most importantly, these special deals can lead to reduced interest rates across all of your loans.

Online tools—the internet revolution

Almost everybody's life has been changed by the internet—if you don't have access to it at work, there's a good chance you have it at home for yourself or your children.

The early online pioneers claimed that everybody would be buying everything online by now. While that turned out to be a little fanciful, the majority of people have still readily adapted to using the internet for many things. We happily do our banking, buy airline tickets, and book accommodation and car hire on the internet. Some people even buy clothes and groceries online as well.

The internet has also been revolutionary for real estate. More and more people see their property for the first time on the internet, using websites such as <realestate.com.au>.

It has also changed the way property finance is handled, by considerably widening competition among lenders. For a start, lenders don't necessarily need to have an office any more because, due to the internet, potential loans can be serviced from anywhere in the country. Even small interstate lenders can now reach investors because of the internet. It seems everyone is selling home loans nowadays.

While it is still possible to physically shop around the banks to try to get a better loan, there is no longer any need to do so. Traipsing from one bank to another in search of a home loan is not only an enormous waste of time, but it is also unlikely to deliver you a spectacularly better deal.

There are plenty of good internet sites on which you can research banking products and interest rates for financing your investment property. Two sites that have been around for a long time and have earned solid reputations are <www.cannex.com. au> and <www.infochoice.com.au>. These informative websites make their profit primarily from selling their data to commercial organisations, and from providing paid research to the media, government and finance professionals.

A quick search through these sites can be illuminating. These websites maintain their independent reputations because financial institutions keep them up to date with every change to their products. If the banks raise or lower interest rates, change product offers or issue new products, these sites are among the first to know because lenders are aware that so many people use them.

There are usually standard formats for displaying information, which makes product comparison between lenders easy — or at least considerably easier than doing it yourself. There are also full tables of current interest rates — which are useful for determining if your home loan interest rate is competitive and who can offer a new customer the most competitive rate.

Another benefit of these sites is their basic online calculating tools, which let you do some number crunching from the comfort of your own home. They have about a dozen calculators to give you an indication of things such as how much you can afford to borrow, what your repayments will be, how much extra repayments or lump sums will save you, how an interest-rate rise will affect your repayments, stamp duty payments, and the usefulness of split loans. There are even calculators that will churn out a list of suburbs in your price range.

There are also other tools to help you budget, work out your income tax and find out how much life insurance you should have (a topic that is covered in chapter 8).

The websites of the major lenders are also great sources of useful information for helping you to understand lending specifics — many have variations on the online calculating tools already mentioned.

Even dedicated property sites, such as <realestate.com.au>, have purchase cost calculators to help work out your finances and total costs when considering how much you should borrow.

You can't do everything online, but half an hour spent browsing a few sites will at least give you an indication of what you should be looking for in terms of interest rates and loan features that might not have existed when you last shopped for a home loan.

Assessing your borrowing risk

Post the recession 'we had to have' in the late 1980s and early 1990s, when interest rates reached approximately 20 per cent, we have had low interest rates. Benign inflation since the mid 1990s has meant low interest rates have been a permanent fixture of the housing market.

This has provided a lot of comfort for property buyers because there have not been wild fluctuations to mortgage repayments. But while steady rates appear to be a feature of the current RBA board's thinking, they are unlikely to last forever.

Borrowing practices have become highly refined. Lenders can, with a high degree of accuracy, roughly predict how many people out of a group of 1000 or 100 000 won't be able to repay their loans. Lenders have developed complex criteria to determine who they will, or won't, take a risk on.

Banks will evict people from of their homes (they have a duty to their shareholders to do so) if they fail to keep up with mortgage repayments; however, because banks know homeowners will sacrifice almost anything to keep their home, they rarely have to. That's one reason why home loan interest rates are lower than rates for other products, like credit cards and car loans.

Until about a decade ago, lenders charged higher interest rates for investment property loans — and some still do. But by and large, investment property loans can be attained at much the same rate as home loans. Nowadays, if you have a home loan on which you are paying 7.5 per cent interest, your lender is likely to offer you financing for your investment property at the same rate.

The repayment buffer

One of the things lenders do to protect themselves and their customers is to determine not only if you can afford the loan now, but also if you could still afford the loan if interest rates were to rise. They include a buffer to give themselves confidence that the customer can handle repayments if interest rates increase (at the time of writing, that buffer tends to be about two percentage points). The example below shows how lenders use this buffer to assess a potential borrower's ability to make repayments.

Example

Let's use amounts based on a 25-year loan, with a current interest rate of 7.5 per cent.

Loan amount	Monthly repayments	
	Actual interest rate 7.5%	Interest rate with buffer 9.5%
$200 000	$1478	$1748
$400 000	$2956	$3495
$600 000	$4434	$5243
$800 000	$5912	$6990
$1 000 000	$7390	$8737

Essentially, lenders assessing you for a loan will not give you a loan unless they are satisfied you can handle servicing the debt even if interest rates rise to 9.5 per cent—which would make repayments more than 18 per cent higher than if they were 7.5 per cent.

The rental income discount

The repayment buffer is the general rule with home loans for owner-occupiers. It is a different situation when you are being assessed for an investment property. Often, with investment properties, the borrower already owns a home or has made a dent in the mortgage. Unlike a home loan, where repayments are met solely from the borrower's income, with investment property there is usually a tenant to help pay the mortgage (through rent). But rather than allowing potential borrowers to just add the rent to their income, banks build in a buffer by applying a discount to the property's rent. It's worth remembering that the rent discounting rule also applies to those investors without their own home.

Lenders discount the property's rent because not all of it ends up in the landlord's pocket — most pay a fee to a real estate agent to manage the property. Landlords also have to pay insurance, rates and maintenance, and there is no guarantee the property will have a tenant all year round.

Handy hint

You should always allow a buffer in your own budgeting for your property to be vacant for about two weeks a year.

Banks generally allow investors to allocate between 60 and 80 per cent of the expected rent towards repaying the loan — and it makes sense. Let's see how it works with one of our previous examples from chapter 4.

Example

In this example we have annual income of $18 200 and two weeks' rent factored in as an expense.

	Income	Expenses
Annual rent	$18 200	
Agent's fees (8%)		$1456
Rates		$700
Insurance		$700
Two weeks vacant (at $350 per week)		$700
Maintenance		$1000
Total	$18 200	$4556

Example *(cont'd)*

The costs of $4556 are 25 per cent of the income of $18 200. Therefore, in our example, the investor would only have about 75 per cent of total potential rent to put towards the mortgage.

Handy hint

If you buy an investment property but you still owe money on your home, make the investment loan interest only. You should concentrate on paying off the principal on your home, because it is not tax deductible. This will maximise tax deductions.

Mortgage brokers

If you haven't applied for a property loan in the past 10 years, there's a good chance the loan process will have changed since your last application. For a start, the mortgage-broking industry means you no longer have to deal directly with a bank.

Brokers now fulfil the job that used to be carried out by the banks' lending managers. Reputable brokers are registered with many lenders (potentially dozens) and can shop around for the best loan for their customer. Good brokers will also take the time to explain products to you.

Handy hint

If you decide to buy an investment property and you haven't been through the loans approval process in recent years, don't just go to your current lender. See a reputable mortgage broker. So many things have changed. You might find that your own bank will lend you the money, but the broker might be able to negotiate a better rate with your existing lender than you could negotiate yourself.

However, the mortgage-broking industry has been criticised for not always being impartial and for being influenced by commissions — ask for a full disclosure of any commissions from the loans being recommended. Overall, the industry is generally reputable.

Remember it's not always the cheapest loan that is the best. You may want or need other features and it may be worth paying a little extra for them, if they will save you money or time.

Becoming a valued bank customer

Everybody knows that buying in bulk saves money. Buy one can of soft drink from the milk bar and it will cost you $2. Buy a box of 24 cans at the supermarket and you may get the whole box for as little as 45 cents a can.

The same applies to banking. If you 'buy' one home loan, then you are no different to thousands of other people; but if you 'buy in bulk' and take out more than one loan, you will make cost savings. The same applies if you need only one credit card, transaction account and cheque book. If you obtain them from different banks, you have established relationships with three separate banks. While in some instances this may work and be cheaper, you will never be a valued customer at any of the banks.

Banks want volume. A customer with a $100 000 loan requires as much effort (paperwork, letters and phone calls) from a lender as a customer with a $1 million loan. But if the bank charges the same interest rate for both customers, it will clearly make about 10 times as much money on the $1 million customer, arguably more. As a result, banks give discounts to customers who borrow larger sums of money — and if they offer the bigger borrower a bit of a discount, he or she might borrow more.

You don't need to have $1 million in loans to get special discounts from banks. All the major banks (ANZ, Commonwealth Bank,

National Australia Bank and Westpac) and most of the second-tier banks (which include St. George, Bank of Queensland, Suncorp Metway, Bendigo Bank, Adelaide Bank and BankWest) offer 'professional package' discounts for business worth as little as $250 000. However, bigger discounts do tend to kick in at points like $500 000 or $700 000.

Each bank has different conditions, but most will also throw in free credit cards, cheque accounts and loyalty programs. Some banks will also waive loan application fees, which is particularly useful if you are planning to build a property portfolio over a number of years.

Anybody who has a mortgage on their home and buys an investment property should never be paying the full mortgage rate — if this is your situation, demand a lower home loan rate.

Handy hint

A colleague had collected about half a dozen loans over the decades —about $1 million in total. They were all charged different interest rates because one was a mortgage, one was a second mortgage, one was for a boat, another was for a car and others were for investment properties. His branch manager had never bothered to tell him that he was a valued customer.

Naturally, he was outraged when told that the interest rates he was paying (there were about six different rates) were ridiculous. Two phone calls (one to a competitor and one to his bank manager) quickly had all his loans on the same rate, saving him about $10 000 a year.

If you have multiple loans for various products, ask your lender for a better rate. Most of the time banks will give you a lower rate because it is cheaper to hold on to one client than it is to find another one if you walk out the door.

Most lenders regularly advertise their 'standard variable rate' (SVR) home loans. Unless you have a small loan (say, less than $150000) and no other significant business with the bank, your bank should offer you a better rate than this. If you have an existing home loan and you are about to buy an investment property, there is a good chance you will have loans in excess of $300000 or, in many cases, $500000. This is enough 'volume' to qualify for discounts of 0.5 per cent to 0.7 per cent off most banks' standard rate.

Valued customers

Matthew and Anne owned their own home outright. They had also used an inheritance to buy an interstate inner-city unit some years ago. In 2000, they bought two more properties in yet another state, using a lender recommended by their developer.

The interest rate charged by the lender wasn't outrageous. But neither was it good. And it certainly didn't reflect the fact that Matthew and Anne now had in excess of $650000 of loans with them (plus another $180000 with another lender). They were paying about 0.03 percentage points below the standard variable rate. By consolidating their loans with another lender, they were able to get all their financing at 0.6 percentage points below the SVR, saving them about $4700 a year.

There was one hidden trap. Their original lender had a break-fee clause (a provision that penalises you if you break the contract after it has been signed), which cost them about $6000 to exit the loans. It was worth it to quit. The $4700 they saved each year effectively paid off the break fee within 16 months, leaving them $4700 better off every year after that. And it paid bigger dividends when they also got the lower rate for another two properties they later bought.

Interest rates — the unknown factor

A property investor has some control over many things that determine the size of a loan. First, there's the decision as to whether you buy a property or not. Second, there's how much is paid for the property and the deposit.

But there is something that individual investors have no control over because they are set by the board of the RBA — interest rates.

The most important determinant of the mortgage interest rates set by banks is the 'official cash rate', which is set by the RBA. The cash rate is the interest rate at which banks lend money to each other for short terms.

Anyone who has had a mortgage for longer than a year or so will know what happens when the RBA decides to play around with interest rates. When rates go up — particularly in the first few years after buying your first home — it can cause financial pain. If you have a $300 000 loan (which is fairly average for a first-home buyer in 2006) and interest rates rise from, say, 7.0 per cent to 7.5 per cent (like the two 0.25 percentage point moves in May and August 2006), the mortgage would rise from $2120 a month to $2217, an increase of $97 a month.

What if there are several increases to the cash rate? Interest rates hit their lowest point in recent times in 2001, when the cash rate in Australia hit 4.25 per cent (soon after the 2001 terrorist attacks in the United States). Since then — remembering that 2001's interest rates were a special case — interest rates have risen seven times, each time by 0.25 percentage points.

If someone had bought a property in early 2001, the interest rate would have been around 6.3 per cent on an average loan of about $230 000. From that time (to the time of writing) interest rates have moved nine times — twice downwards and seven times upwards. In that case, the principal and interest repayments on that sum would have initially been about $1524 a month. Later that year they would have fallen to $1454 a month before rising to around $1670 — an increase of $146 a month. Yes, that's a lot of extra money. But it also happened over a period of five years and most people's incomes would have risen a little over that time — and there were plenty of warnings that interest rates were at unsustainable, historic lows.

The point is this: interest rates move up and down. They've been as high as above 20 per cent in the early 1990s, during the last major recession. They have also twice dropped to below about 6 per cent. After the rate rise in August 2006, the average interest rate being paid by a homebuyer was around 7.5 per cent.

The fluctuations of interest rates are one of the risks associated with property investment and should not be ignored. If rates rise too high, too fast, some investors may have to sell properties at a time that is not particularly convenient — and selling into a falling market can often be scarier than facing increased mortgage rates.

Fixed interest rates

Then there are fixed interest rates. This is an option that banks often market to people who have concerns, or even fears, that interest rates will rise quickly. Fixed interest rates are designed to give buyers peace of mind — you will know exactly how much your repayments are for the period of the loan.

However, investors will tend to pay a small premium for fixed interest rates. At most points in the cycle, fixed rates are usually a bit higher than variable loan rates and can be a gamble for investors. Sometimes, when banks believe official interest rates are likely to fall quickly, fixed rates may be set below the variable rates. Over the course of a full cycle of rates rising and falling, however, banks will tend to have some sort of a premium built in for fixed rates. And most of the time, the banks will win.

Sometimes you can both save money and beat the banks — but it is a complex risk that will usually involve more luck than skill.

But despite the fact that you are playing money games against a bank, fixed interest rates can still make sense for some investors. If your concern about rising interest rates is strong, then you may be able to sleep better at night knowing that you have guaranteed interest payments for a set period. Fixed rates don't change for the term of a loan — whether it is six months or 10 years. They mean that investors have certainty for the period for which they took out the loan — and that can make investors less anxious about their financial future.

More than one wise property sage has said that if you see a long-term fixed interest rate that you think is reasonable and would give you certainty, then why not sign up for it? While it takes a lot of the ongoing and unknown concerns out of property investment, you need to be aware of the trade-off. Fixed interest rates will probably cost you more, but they could be worthwhile just for the certainty they bring.

Preparing a business plan

Often of more importance than securing your finance, is ensuring that you can actually afford the property you are planning to buy — and a business plan will help you do this. A business plan is not much different to a budget — be it for a household or for a whole country — in that it shows money coming in and money going out. However, for business plans you will also need to do some projections and estimates.

The basic information required for a business plan includes:

▲   the property's total purchase costs

▲   estimated holding expenses (such as interest, maintenance, management, insurance and rates)

▲   estimated income from the property

▲ all your other income

▲ all your other expenses (personal and household)

▲ a timeline of your income and expenses (a year planner in most diaries is handy for this) and when they are received and paid.

A strong business plan will spell out in black and white what your proposed investment is going to cost and exactly how and when you will be able to meet the bills (known as your cash flow).

Cash flow

Although receiving a tax refund or reduced tax at the end of the financial year is a great bonus for negatively geared investments, it is pretty useless if you can't afford to pay the ongoing expenses throughout the year.

To accurately predict your cash flow, your business plan should include a personal finance timeline and a property investment timeline.

The first thing your personal finance timeline will show you is how much extra spending power you will have each year — before you even buy any investment property. It will detail your income and expenses and provide a timeline of when you will need extra funds during the year (such as at Christmas and holidays). It will show you when you are pushed for money (you might find that you have a particular month where you have an avalanche of bills).

Your property investment timeline will do the same thing, by showing estimated income and expenses and when they are due. By matching up the two timelines you can quickly see how the investment is going to affect your cash flow.

Ideally, you should set up regular expenses to be paid on a monthly or quarterly basis throughout the year, for both your personal finances and your property investment—which will reduce the peaks and troughs and provide a steady cash-flow position all year long.

Documents the bank will want to see

To help ensure that the approval process for your loan runs smoothly, start collecting, in advance, the documents the bank will want to see. These are usually proof of income, proof of expenses and proof of the value of any security you are offering.

The documents you may need to show the bank include:

▲ last two consecutive pay slips

▲ proof of any other regular income

▲ last two years' tax returns (especially self-employed people)

▲ last three months' credit card statements

▲ details of all existing borrowings (personal, car, investment, mortgages)

▲ rates notice or valuation on existing property to be used as security

▲ details of other assets and proof of ownership

▲ details of superannuation accounts and assets.

Most of these documents must also be originals—not photocopies—or, at least, notarised copies (copies signed by a Justice of the Peace or other approved person). Organising this paperwork can take a couple of weeks to get together, so it will help if you are prepared.

Once you have signed a contract to buy a property and you know the exact amount of money you want to borrow, you will also need to give the lender copies of:

▲ the contract

▲ any other associated documents

▲ your lawyer's or conveyancer's contact details.

In many cases you can apply for a loan over the internet and you will never have to physically visit the bank. Once your online application has been received, the lender will mail out the mortgage documents for your signature, along with other permission forms such as a repayment schedule, direct debit authorities, settlement or closure approvals.

The next thing you know, you will be a mortgagee again!

Chapter 8

Doing the legals and insuring the property

In this chapter we will cover the following:

▲ Presale documentation

▲ Building and pest inspections

▲ The contract

▲ Conveyancing

▲ Taxes, fees and charges

▲ Lenders' mortgage insurance

▲ Land tax

▲ Insurance.

The act of investing has undergone some significant, if not radical, changes in the past decade. For instance, if you want to invest in shares, you don't even need to know a stockbroker, let alone contact one. The advent of online stock-trading companies means you can buy shares from the comfort of your internet-enabled home. And, if you know what stock you want, you can buy and sell for about $20 to $30 a transaction without getting anyone else involved.

While the internet has changed property investment, it is not yet as simple as buying shares online. Property, being the tangible asset that it is, will probably always require a level of personal involvement and interaction. Most investors will want to visit a potential investment property and make judgements on whether it's the right property for them.

True, you can find the house you want to buy online. You could probably even call the agent and make a bid for it over the phone (this is becoming more common). But, because every property is different, few people buy their first home, or investment property, without physically walking through the property.

That is one major reason why investment in property and investment in shares are fundamentally different. Company shares are homogenous—each share is the same as the next.

Real estate is not uniform—no two properties can be the same. Even large blocks of apartments will contain apartments that are different. Every property in the world is unique. And just as every property has its own identity, so too does every property have its own legal status and is recognised by the local council as a piece of land in its own right.

Presale documentation

The first document you're likely to see before buying a property is the promotional material that gives a snapshot of it. This could be via the internet, a newspaper, a brochure in your letterbox or a property magazine produced by a real estate agent. It will contain the barest, but the most effective, information for enticing potential buyers to look at the property.

Once you've found a property you think you might be interested in, ask the real estate agent (or developer or vendor) for any presale documentation (including the contract). Presale documentation goes by different names in different states. For instance, Victoria has what is known as a 'Vendor's statement' or 'Section 32' and there is a separate 'Contract of sale'. In New South Wales, it is simply called the 'Contract for sale'. Queensland sales agents are required to give prospective buyers the 'PAMD Form 27c disclosure to buyer' and a 'PAMD Form 30c warning statement', which informs them of their right to a cooling-off period. In the ACT, the presale documentation (usually in the sale contract itself) must also include an 'Energy Efficiency Rating' (EER).

Whatever it's called in your state, the documents contain vital information that should be checked over by a legal representative. While the legal requirements of the presale documentation differ between states and territories, it will include general and specific information relevant to the property (for example, rates notices for the property, the size and location of the land, any covenants on the property, or previous mortgages).

As there are different legal requirements in each state, you should check that your presale documentation is correct with your state government website or state office of the REIA.

Building and pest inspections

Unless you are an experienced builder, how would you know what to look for to ascertain whether a house is structurally deficient? Unless you are a pest inspector how would you know if there is a major termite problem? Building inspection and pest inspection reports (also known as pre-purchase inspection reports) are very important elements of the buying process. Some buyers don't bother to get them, which can be risky.

Owner-occupiers will often be aware of the problems in their house, but have learnt to live with them or could not afford, or be bothered, to fix them. Many of these problems are not automatically obvious. Often, it is only after much time has been spent living in a house that faults become obvious.

Inspections can also become a part of the negotiation process. If there is serious work required for the property, then perhaps the price of the property can be negotiated. Would you still pay the same price for a house if you knew it was going to require $10 000, $20 000 or $30 000 worth of important work in the next three years? Possibly, but it would be nice to know about it first — and it could be ammunition for talking down the asking price of the property under negotiation.

If you were to show the vendor of a potential investment property a building inspection report that shows how neglected the house is, you might find he or she is more willing to accept a lower price. How much lower? Well, it's still up to the vendor, and he or she will want as high a price as possible, but in some circumstances, it could be a handy negotiating tool.

Building and pest inspection reports are often carried out as separate inquiries, producing separate reports. Some firms will do both for you. They usually cost a few hundred dollars ($250 to $400 each), depending on how competitive things are in your area.

Building inspections

What the building inspection report reveals about an older property will depend on the love and attention it has received over the years. The older the property, the more ongoing work it will need to keep the 'body' in shape. For instance, old properties with solid 'wet' plaster will almost certainly have cracks in the walls. But cracks don't necessarily mean that the house is about to fall over or that there are potentially serious problems with the structure. It could just mean that a particularly wet or dry period has caused a temporary problem with the soil, causing movements in the foundations that have led to cracking.

Other issues a building inspector might uncover include asbestos, rising damp, problems with the structure, quality of the roof, guttering, downpipes and electrical wiring. Building inspectors should also give an indication of how much it will cost to fix any problems and how soon the work will be required.

Pest inspections

Pest inspections are important for identifying any property damage caused by pests. The most obvious culprits are termites. They can leave floorboards flaky and dangerous, or eat away at timber frames that are the basis of your walls or roof trusses. Even solid brick homes can have termites.

It is important to note that with properties bought at auction, the buyer is unable to put conditions on the sale. Therefore, inspections should be carried out about a week or more before the auction date to give the inspectors time to write their reports and for you to have time to read them properly.

It is different with properties bought privately (private sales are covered in chapter 6). In this instance, you can wait until after you have agreed on a price and then make the contract 'subject to' satisfactory building and pest inspections. However, if there is strong competition for the property, it is probably best to have your reports in hand before making an offer. That way, you will then have all the facts at your fingertips in case you need to make a counteroffer. If two buyers make similar offers — with one offer being conditional and the other unconditional — a wise seller will usually accept the unconditional offer.

The contract

Depending on how you bought the property, the contract of sale, or contract, will be signed soon after you verbally agree on a price with the vendor (usually through the agent). It contains a number of important elements, including the agreed price, the deposit to be paid, the date at which ownership will change (known as settlement), the property's fixtures and fittings and what chattels are included.

Chattels are items like curtains, blinds, dishwashers (if easily detachable), pool equipment, transportable garden sheds and plants in the garden that are not necessarily a part of the property, but that the owner is likely to include with the sale.

Fixtures and fittings are permanent and come with the property and include light fixtures, dishwashers (if plumbed in), ovens, floor tiles, built-in cupboards and wardrobes.

As already mentioned earlier in this chapter, the contract may also include conditions on the sale (such as building inspections or subject to finance being approved).

If you have not had a lawyer look over documents relating to the house, now is definitely the time to get one, particularly if you have bought by private treaty. Most states have a cooling-off period (usually of at least a few days) when houses are bought privately. You should arrange for your legal adviser to receive a copy of the contract as soon as possible. Agents will usually arrange this for you, but don't rely on them to do so. You may only have a few days for your lawyer to look at the contract before the cooling-off period ends, and if the agent does not provide you with the contract in time, you will lose your cooling-off period.

If you are buying in Victoria, there is also what is known as a 'contract note'. A contract note is not the contract of sale itself, but it is still commonly used by real estate agents. Some argue that it is simply another selling tool for real estate agents — one that can be dangerous for vendors and purchasers because it diverts their attention from the actual contract of sale, prepared by the vendor's lawyer. It gives agents the power to dictate the terms of purchase. If you want to make the sale conditional, make sure you have those conditions listed clearly to your own satisfaction on the contract note, no matter what the agent says. If the agent won't let you add conditions to their contract note, don't sign it — otherwise you may find that you lose legal rights.

Conveyancing

Conveyancing involves the legal transfer of property. It involves checking the legitimacy of titles, transferring ownership, making sure the correct taxes/duties are paid to various governments and that funds are transferred between the buyer and seller.

It is possible to do your own conveyancing — books have been written on the topic and do-it-yourself conveyancing kits are also available. But most people leave it to the experts — lawyers and specialist conveyancing firms — because unless you know what you're doing, it will be time consuming and risky.

There is also plenty of debate about whether you should get lawyers or conveyancers to do the job. While lawyers argue that conveyancers don't offer the same level of legal protection, conveyancers claim that a lawyer's legal protection provides better protection for the lawyer than it does for the client. One important difference between the two, however, is that because conveyancers are not lawyers, they are not legally allowed to offer advice on the purchase of the property (although many do anyway). Because lawyers can give advice, they argue that they can offer a more robust service. Lawyers will also generally be able to give you ongoing legal advice for matters other than the conveyancing. And, like having a good accountant, property investors should always have a lawyer they can call on when required.

When it comes to fees, there is little difference between the two service providers nowadays. Fees for conveyancing do, however, vary considerably and are usually somewhere between $300 and $1000.

The Power of Property

Whether you choose a lawyer or a conveyancer, the person doing your conveyancing is required to make sure that there are no nasty hidden surprises that come with the property. Many properties will have legal restraints (such as easements), or zoning conditions or restrictions on the title or use of the property. Buyers need to know about these in advance, so that they don't, for example, buy a warehouse with the intention of turning it into apartments, only to find the local council will not allow residential developments on that piece of land.

Taxes, fees and charges

State governments make a lot of money from the real estate industry. Taxes and charges are added to all manner of things associated with property — and stamp duty is one of them.

Stamp duty is the single biggest cost — after the property itself — involved in buying a house. Each state and territory has its own system for charging stamp duties, with some states also having various exemptions. Victoria, for example, has a specific discount on stamp duty where the property is bought off the plan. You should contact your State Revenue Office for details.

However, stamp duty is just one of a number of charges that state governments place on properties. In some states, there are also mortgage registration fees, transfer fees and another stamp duty, which is charged according to the size of the mortgage.

In total, these taxes will usually add between 3 and 5 per cent to the cost of a property, depending on the state. Our example below shows the extra cost of stamp duty for each state.

Example

For this example, we'll use a property worth $300000 and assume the total loan is also for $300000 (although investors can normally add the costs of these taxes and other buying costs to their loan).

State	Stamp duty for a $300 000 purchase
ACT	$9 500
NSW	$8 990
NT	$12 150
Qld	$9 475
SA	$11 330
Tas	$9 550
Vic	$13 660
WA	$10 700

There are many other costs that differ between the states, but for a $300 000 house and loan, the main ones include a mortgage registration fee (between about $45 and $110), transfer fee ($90 to $1600), and a stamp duty on the loan ($0 to about $1200). There are also other costs that will be incurred and charged back to you by your conveyancer.

Then there are 'settlement offsets', which square up the ledger for bills the previous owner paid in advance (such as council property rates, water rates, body corporate fees and insurances). You should expect to pay a few hundred dollars in offsets.

Your bank, or mortgage lender, may also charge you a fee for your loan and for attending to the property settlement.

Lenders' mortgage insurance

Of all the costs associated with buying a property, this one is the nastiest. Lenders' mortgage insurance (LMI) is a sum the bank charges if you don't have enough equity in your property (or your property portfolio). LMI is generally charged by banks when the value of your loan, or loans, exceeds 80 per cent of the value of your property or properties.

But the insurance doesn't cover you. It covers your lender. That's right: the lender takes out insurance in case you default on your mortgage, but it makes you pay the premium. If you fall into a financial hole (like losing your job or becoming ill) and are unable to repay your loan and the bank has to sell your house, LMI will cover the bank if it loses money when your house is sold.

However, people who own their home and are looking to buy an investment property are less likely to have to pay LMI because banks will usually take into account their entire property portfolio. If you have some equity in your own home, you might be able to borrow the entire value of an investment property (plus extra costs, taking the loan up to 110 per cent of the value of the investment property) and not have to pay LMI.

Example

Let's say Steven and Michelle bought their house five years ago and have paid down their loan to $120000, while, at the same time, their house increased in value to $400000. They now want to buy an investment property valued at $320000 and want to borrow the entire amount, plus fees and charges, which means they need an investment loan of $336000. The value of their two properties is $720000. The value of their loans is $456000, or 63.3 per cent of the value of the two properties. They are unlikely to have to pay LMI in this case, as their loans are substantially less than the 80 per cent level at which a lender will generally seek LMI.

However, if they had not had as much equity in their own home, they could well have had to face paying LMI.

If the value of your loans is only a little bit over 80 per cent, you may also find that a bit of negotiation with your lender, particularly if you have been with them for a while, could see the LMI waived.

Land tax

Land tax is another complicated tax charged by most states and territories. It is an annual tax charged on the unimproved land value of a property, which means the value of the land not including any structures on it.

It can also be charged on the total of all your landholdings, known as the 'multiple holding basis'. For example, an investor might have an investment property worth $300 000, where the land is valued at $150 000. This holding might fall below the state's land tax threshold. However, when he or she buys a second investment property, if the value of the total landholdings rises over a state's threshold, land tax will apply. While each property may be below the threshold for land tax, when the two properties are added together they will trigger the tax. The one upside of this impost is that, unlike stamp duties, it is an immediate tax deduction against your income.

Also, being a state tax, the cumulative effect is only calculated on land holdings in that particular state. Diversifying your property portfolio across several different states could therefore assist you in avoiding state land taxes.

The list of exemptions in each state is long. Most states have thresholds under which the tax is not payable, while some have exemptions for the principal place of residence and have different rules for companies or trusts. Again, you will need an accountant to tell you more about land tax in your state, or you could find it on the internet through your state government's revenue office.

Insurance

There is possibly nothing more dangerous than buying a house without properly covering the insurable risks. What are the insurance risks inherent with investment property? How about the house burning down? How about tenants destroying the property and making it uninhabitable without extensive work? How about somebody injuring themselves on your property? What happens to the investment if you die? What happens if you have an accident and can't work yourself?

The chance of any of those things happening is quite low; however, if any of them did happen and you weren't insured, the financial consequences could be devastating. Banks will often require that you have insurance when they lend you money to protect their investment. But anyone who thinks they can go into property investment without taking out some insurance for themselves probably shouldn't be getting into property investment in the first place.

The good news about most general insurance — including home and contents, landlord and public liability — is that it is generally tax deductible.

House and contents insurance

As soon as you sign a contract to buy, you have an insurable interest in that property. If the house burns down — even before settlement — you could lose money. For a start, you have no guarantee that the vendor has insurance. So the minimum you need is house and contents insurance — enough to cover completely rebuilding the house, including carpets, light fittings, curtains, ovens, sheds, garages and other items, such as clothes lines. Your insurance should be enough to cover you to completely rebuild again if you were given the same block of land with nothing on it. It should also cover clearing the site itself, architects fees, planning permits and building permits — most insurers offer this as part of their regular policy.

Handy hint

Spend a few minutes reviewing each of your insurance policies every year because some details change annually. Building costs might have risen sharply, or the rent you earn might have increased. Alternatively, the insurer might have increased some figures on your policy beyond what would be reasonable. It can't hurt to check and it could save you money.

Landlord's insurance

The next insurance to consider is landlord's insurance, which can often be taken out as an addition to a home and contents policy. Under certain specified conditions, the insurance company will continue to pay the rent if the tenant can't, or won't. It can be a natural extension of the building burning down. Remember that if the house doesn't exist, the tenant is unlikely to be paying rent!

Some landlord's insurance policies will also cover the situation where a tenant refuses to pay the rent but continues to live in the property, or where the tenant (or the tenant's visitors) steals from the landlord by taking items that are part of the house when the tenancy ends. Some policies will also cover your legal costs if you need to kick your tenants out.

Handy hint

Find yourself an insurance broker when you buy an investment property. Not only will you need insurance for the new property you've bought, but a broker might be able to save you a lot of money with your other insurance policies, like your car or home and contents insurance.

Public liability insurance

Another important type of insurance is public liability insurance, which is also largely offered in conjunction with the home and contents policy. It is mainly used to cover accidents (whether they were caused by you or someone else) that may occur on your property.

Public liability insurance is usually intended for very large sums, like $5 million to $20 million, but it is also designed to cover your legal expenses and any potential damages claims made against you for accidents on your property.

Types of life insurance

Something that often gets forgotten in discussions about property are the types of insurance — life, total and permanent disablement, trauma, and income protection — that come under life insurance.

Most people who get into property investment are doing so to secure their own future and that of their family. But what happens if you die soon after you start investing in property? Or if you buy your second or third investment property but you have $1 million worth of debt? What happens if you have a serious accident and you can't work again?

If you have decided to build a property portfolio in the hope of building an asset base for the future, then it could be catastrophic if something happened to you.

The four types of life insurance are too complex to go into great detail here, but let us go through a few scenarios.

Death cover

Life insurance is a lump sum that is paid out on death. If one partner dies, the lump sum could be used to pay out your own home mortgage and any other investment property mortgages you might have. If you have $500 000 of life insurance (say, $200 000 for the home and $300 000 for investment property debt), then your partner could pay out the mortgage and would still receive the rent from the investment property. This could be particularly important when multiple properties are involved.

Total and permanent disability insurance

This is also a lump sum (that cannot be more than the total of life insurance taken out) that is paid out when certain injuries or illnesses stop you from working for a period of, generally, six months or longer. Total and permanent disability insurance could be helpful if you lose an eye, arm or a leg. It could keep you afloat while you recover and also greatly reduce the need to sell properties.

Trauma insurance

Another lump-sum payment, trauma insurance is designed to pay out when you survive illnesses. Previously, illnesses like cancer, strokes and heart attacks were much more likely to be terminal. Nowadays, although modern medicine means a greater chance of survival, you could be left with monstrous medical bills, plus a need to spend a large sum of money renovating a house to make it easier for you to live in or gain access to.

Income protection insurance

Income protection insurance will provide an ongoing income payable if you are unable to work for extended periods. Generally, income protection will cover up to 75 per cent of the insured's income. If he or she earns $80 000 a year, up to $60 000 a year in income-protection payments could be received. This would be very important for property investors, particularly the self-employed, if they found themselves unable to work for an extended period (say, six months) because of an accident.

If an investor's property plan relied on continuing to receive an annual salary—and that would be nearly all investors, but particularly negatively geared investors—then the plan would be shot if the income stopped coming in.

Income protection insurance is the most complex and most expensive. There are many variables, including age, occupation and length of coverage. It is, however, tax deductible, because the income you receive in the event of a claim would be taxed as income.

Financial tip

Cover yourself properly with life and income protection insurance. If you buy a second or third or fourth property and you intend those properties to look after your family in years to come, it would be counterproductive if, due to your death or a serious illness, the very properties you bought to protect you and your family had to be prematurely sold because you could no longer afford to keep them.

Life insurance is complex. Investors should get advice from a licensed life insurance broker about their individual needs.

Chapter 9

The tax man will help you

In this chapter we will cover the following:

▲ What is an allowable expense?

▲ The shoebox — don't laugh, it's true!

▲ What you can claim now

▲ Interest

▲ What you can claim later — depreciation

▲ Putting it all together.

It may sound a little too good to be true, but tenants aren't the only ones who will help you meet the financial costs associated with your investment property — the tax man will also help. Considering his reputation for penny-pinching, it may be a little difficult for you to believe that the tax man will lend you a helping hand — and sometimes he will even lend you two.

With his left hand, he will hand you back some money to compensate you for some of the expenses you incurred in your investment. This will be a portion of what you spent on costs like agent's fees, insurance and council rates.

While with his right hand — in some cases — he will let you claim an amount when the value of the costs incurred in building and furnishing your property reduce (also known as depreciation). This is not to be confused with the value of the investment itself, which is hopefully appreciating.

What is an allowable expense?

The Australian Government, through the ATO, allows investors to claim the cost of maintaining an income-producing investment. For owners of property, that means most costs legitimately incurred as a result of investment in property can be claimed as an expense.

According to the ATO, there are three types of expenses for rental properties: those you can claim immediately (in the current tax year); those you have to claim in the future (in subsequent tax years); and those you can never claim.

Typically, the types of expenses that you can never claim are those that you didn't incur yourself in the first place. These include the costs of electricity and water charged to and paid by the tenant.

Investors are also not allowed to claim the costs associated with buying and selling property — costs such as conveyancing, advertising expenses, stamp duty and the cost of the property itself. However, these will, in most cases, become defacto expenses when a property is sold, as they become part of the capital base for working out any CGT paid on the profit from selling the property (see chapter 15 for more details).

The other general costs that cannot be claimed are costs incurred when the property is not available for rent or is partly used by you, such as a holiday home. If the property is partly for your own use, you can't claim the portion of time in which you use it (see chapter 12 for more on holiday homes), or when it is not available for rent.

The shoebox — don't laugh, it's true!

When it comes to owning shares or bonds, you might occasionally have to fill in a little bit of paperwork, such as board-election forms and bank account numbers for dividend payments. Investment property is not like most other investments. There can be a lot of paperwork. You could have it all done by your accountant, but that would be expensive if you had to pay by the hour.

If you're not a good filer of records but want to be a property investor, then you'd better get into the habit. Get yourself a box (a decent-sized shoebox is the perfect size) and put all your property paperwork in it as you receive it. When your agent sends you the monthly rent statement, put it in the shoebox. When your bank sends your loan account statement, put that in there also — put all of your records in it. Once you make the action automatic, it won't be a chore. It will also mean that you will have all your records at your fingertips when it's time to visit your accountant. Just put everything related to your property in the shoebox and sort it out at the end of the financial year.

What you can claim now

The good news is that the list of things for which the ATO will let you claim an immediate deduction is pretty sensible. In some cases, it's also quite generous.

Apart from interest, which is the most obvious and biggest expense that you can generally claim immediately (we will deal with this later in the chapter), the next biggest ongoing cost is likely to be your managing agent, if you choose to employ one. Some agents charge a fee for everything, which can get quite complicated. However, the general rule for residential property is that they will charge an ongoing fee of between 5 and 8 per cent (for properties let to a single tenant for extended periods).

Most agents also charge a fee for finding you a tenant, usually between one and two weeks' rent, to cover the agency's time in opening the house for inspection. This fee may or may not include advertising costs. (If advertising costs are charged separately, they can also be claimed.)

The other big and obvious items that can be claimed immediately are council rates, insurances and body corporate fees (as long as the fee is not a special payment for building works, which becomes a capital expense). The importance of fully insuring your property cannot be overstated (it is covered in chapter 8).

Ongoing maintenance is probably the last of the regular expenses. Gardening (it is a rare and precious tenant that looks after a garden), or repairing the hot-water system, oven, a leaky roof or a broken TV antenna, or fixing a host of things that can go wrong can generally be claimed as ongoing maintenance. (Incidentally, because you can claim maintenance costs against your tax, it makes it cheaper than getting the same work done on your own home.)

Yet it doesn't end there. You can also claim other expenses, including bank charges, cleaning, legal expenses, land tax, or bookkeeping, accounting and secretarial fees, and travel costs associated with inspecting or maintaining your property.

For an up-to-date and comprehensive list of the ATO's claimable expenses for rental properties, visit the ATO or go to its website and download the relevant booklet, <www.ato.gov.au/content/downloads/NAT1729-06.pdf>.

Handy hint

There has been a significant increase in the number of property investors over the past decade. In 2004, the ATO raised concerns about the total amount of deductions being claimed by investors. It launched a crackdown, which is ongoing. Simply, stick to the rules of what you can and can't claim and don't try to artificially inflate your claims.

When it comes to knowing what you can and can't claim, we highly recommend that you use a reputable and experienced accountant.

Interest

In the first few years of owning an investment property, loan interest is likely to be the largest expense you incur. Often, but not always, it will dwarf all the rent received for the property (making the property negatively geared).

When you buy a property with borrowed money, you will usually have a choice to pay interest only or principal and interest. Only the interest component is a claimable expense.

Whether you opt for an interest-only or a principal-and-interest loan is an individual decision and will depend on your attitude to debt. Purely from a tax perspective, it makes more sense to pay interest only, particularly if you have other personal, non–tax-deductible debt (like your home). This is because non–tax-deductible investment debt enables you to claim the interest paid on the investment as a tax deduction — up to 46.5 per cent of the interest. This cannot be done with your principal residence.

However, an interest-only loan will not suit all people; some investors will want to see the equity in their investment property grow faster, so that while the property is appreciating, the loan is also decreasing because the principal is being repaid.

To claim the entire year's interest payments, the house must be available to rent for the entire year — this is particularly relevant if you want to use your property for a holiday home. When it comes to vacant blocks of land, the ATO says that interest is deductible if the owner has the 'intention' to develop the property. If you are intending to buy vacant land and hold it for some years before developing it, you will need an accountant to properly advise you.

What you can claim later — depreciation

Not all expenses for an investment property can be claimed as a tax deduction in the same year the expense was incurred. There are three general types of items that fit into this category — borrowing costs, depreciating assets and capital works items.

Borrowing costs include fees and charges involved in setting up a loan. If they are more than $100, they are written down over five years — meaning that 20 per cent of the cost can be claimed each year for five years.

The other two expenses that can be claimed later — depreciating assets and capital works — are quite complex issues. The basic reasoning behind both of them is that most assets have a lifespan and depreciate in value over that lifespan.

Asset depreciation

Asset depreciation means that instead of getting an up-front deduction for an item such as $3000 worth of carpets, the ATO will make you claim the cost over a period of 10 years, as it has deemed it takes about 10 years for carpet to become worthless.

To further complicate matters, there are two different methods for depreciating assets — the prime-cost method and the diminishing-value method. However, because each depreciable item in a property has a different lifespan, we can't deal with all of them here. (Accountants deal with these issues on a daily basis and will be able to advise you in full.)

Demonstrating the complexity of depreciation rules, the ATO's *Rental Properties Guide 2006* contains the lifespans of more than 230 depreciable items and information about how they can be depreciated. The guide is available from the ATO, or it can be downloaded from its website, <www.ato.gov.au/content/downloads/NAT1729-06.pdf>.

Table 9.1 shows the lifespans of seven depreciable assets, as listed in the *Rental Properties Guide 2006*:

Table 9.1: lifespans of depreciating assets

Item	Lifespan (years)
Carpet	10
Hot-water system (gas or electric)	12
Hot-water system (solar)	15
Rugs	7
Smoke alarms	6
Dishwashers and microwaves	10
Ovens and stoves	12

Source: Australian Taxation Office (ATO)

Depreciation is a crucial part of property investing. While spending money on your property is important, for both attracting and retaining tenants, proper recording of purchased items can also make a big difference to managing the cash flow of your property. This is particularly important for owners of older properties where a number of items need to be upgraded over a longer period. In addition, investors who let out partly or fully furnished flats should also have some knowledge of asset depreciation rules — and keep accurate records of depreciable items.

It's also worth remembering that you do not have to have personally bought the items after you purchased your property — items that were part of the property when you bought it can be depreciated.

Handy hint

It is a good idea when you buy a property to call in a depreciation expert (look under 'valuers — real estate' in a phone directory) to give you a depreciation schedule for your property. This is especially important in new properties, where there could be thousands of dollars of claims a year. Sometimes with new properties, the developers will already have a prepared depreciation schedule that includes all the items they installed and used, along with the items' costs and dates. It will cost about $400 to $700 (but is a tax deduction) and should pay for itself in the first year or two.

Asset depreciation and its effect on your income

Here is a recent example of the depreciation schedule of a five-year-old, three-bedroom weatherboard house. A depreciation expert was hired and assessed the items in the house and, by estimating their original purchase price, drew up the depreciation schedule shown in table 9.2.

With the exception of the light fittings (with a lifespan of 13 years) and the carpet (a lifespan 10 years), the remaining items have a 20-year lifespan, according to the ATO. The depreciation schedule gives total depreciating assets of $10 210. After apportioning the correct annual depreciation amount for each asset, the investor is able to claim $741.25 a year for the next five years (but after five years the amount will reduce because the carpet's effective life will be finished). This comes off the investor's annual taxable income.

Table 9.2: depreciation schedule

Item	Original value
TV aerial	$150
Gas hot-water service	$790
Curtains	$800
Oven	$950
Light fittings	$850
Ducted heating unit	$1750
Range hood and fans	$450
Hot plates	$270
Carpets/tiles	$4200

The investor will get a portion of that $741.25 back on tax. If the investor is on the 31.5 per cent marginal tax rate (including the Medicare levy), he or she would get back approximately $222.38, while someone on the highest marginal tax rate (46.5 per cent) would get back $344.68. We will show this in more detail at the end of the chapter.

....

Did you know?

Also explained in the ATO's *Rental Properties Guide 2006* is the tax treatment if you buy a number of low-value items. Items that cost less than $300 can generally be claimed in entirety in the first year. Items bought for between $300 and $1000 are generally put into a 'low-value pool'. The ATO will then allow a much more rapid depreciation rate.

....

Building depreciation (capital works)

While depreciating fixtures and fittings is very important from a cash flow perspective, we've left the biggest depreciating asset until last.

In 1985, the government tinkered with depreciation laws. It introduced a sweetener for residential property investors, allowing them to depreciate the value of the house itself (also known as capital works deduction). Previously, there was no allowable depreciation for the cost of normal residential rental property. Depending on the date construction commenced, investors can depreciate the value of the bricks and mortar over a period of either 25 or 40 years.

If construction on the property began between 18 July 1985 and 15 September 1987 (a small window of time), the building can be depreciated at 4 per cent a year over 25 years. However, there are comparatively few properties that hold this depreciation allowance, because the period for which the 25-year rule applies only lasted two years.

If construction started after 15 September 1987, the building can be depreciated at 2.5 per cent a year over 40 years. As this rule has been around for nearly two decades, we will concentrate on this one.

What is included in building depreciation? Essentially, it is costs such as the bricks and mortar, the timber framework, any extensions (such as extra bedrooms and bathrooms), driveways, carports, retaining walls and swimming pools.

While depreciation of the other assets in the house will, in most cases, be less than $20 000 for an entire house, construction costs are quite high. Building a standard new three-bedroom house in 2006 may cost somewhere between $110 000 and $250 000 (although it can certainly cost much more than that!).

Building depreciation and its effect on your income

Let's look at a property built in 2006 for a capital works budget of $130 000. The investor who purchased the property would be able to depreciate 2.5 per cent of $130 000. That means he or she can claim a deduction for $3250 each year for the next 40 years.

Because this is a sum that reduces your income — without really having to pay for it up-front — you will effectively get a return according to your marginal tax rate. For the average wage earner (31.5 per cent marginal tax rate), a tax return of $1023.75 year would be available, while for someone on the 46.5 per cent rate (including the Medicare levy), a return of $1511.25 would apply.

Building depreciation, because of the comparatively large sums involved, can have a powerful effect on the cash flow of your property, particularly over a longer period. However, it is an argument that divides property 'experts'. In order to get the building depreciation, you need to buy new houses — in some ways, the newer the better. Others claim that older homes, particularly period styles, will have superior capital growth Although any improvement work you conduct on an older home can be depreciated.

For most investors, particularly in the early stages of building a property portfolio, buying a relatively new building is something to consider. The value of the write-down off income is effectively like receiving extra rent — but its value depends on your marginal tax rate. The tax system essentially 'rewards' investors on higher incomes more than it does those on lower incomes — fair or not, that's how our tax system works.

Building depreciation and capital gains tax

There is one more important issue to note with the capital works deduction. As you depreciate the property, it will affect the cost base of the property itself—meaning that when you sell the property, you will have to pay a higher amount of CGT.

Let's assume an investor bought a property for $250 000 and the capital value of the building works was valued at $100 000 at the time it was built.

Our investor holds the property for four years, over which time he or she claims $10 000 ($100 000 × 2.5% × 4 years). That reduces the cost base of the property from $250 000 to $240 000. The investor sells the property after year four for $320 000. Although the profit is $70 000 ($320 000 less $250 000), he or she will have to pay tax on $80 000 ($320 000 less the written-down cost base of $240 000). So, the depreciated amount is used for working out the profit for CGT purposes.

It may seem like claiming an allowance only to pay it back later—but it doesn't quite work this way.

The investor is claiming the original depreciation amount of $2500 a year ($10 000 over four years) at his or her marginal tax rate. But when the property is sold, only half the investor's capital gain is taxed (if the investment is held for more than one year).

Let's assume our investor in the above example was on the top marginal tax rate. Over the four years that he or she claimed the building depreciation allowance, a total of $4650 was received back on tax for depreciation (46.5 per cent of $10 000). But the cost base has now fallen from $250 000 to $240 000. Had our investor not claimed the depreciation allowance, he or she would pay CGT on the $70 000, rather than $80 000. If the asset was held for more than one year, only half the gain is added to his or her income. So, without claiming the allowance, the investor would have to pay $16 275 ($70 000 × 0.5 × 46.5%). If the depreciation allowance was claimed, he or she would have to pay $18 600 ($80 000 × 0.5 × 46.5%).

The extra CGT that our investor has paid is $2325; however, along the way, he or she received tax returns totaling $4650. Our investor is still $2325 ahead — even though a higher amount of CGT had to be paid, he or she really only had to pay back about half of the amount claimed.

Putting it all together

So, let's put this whole depreciation issue into context. Yes, depreciation is complex, but what we hope you will understand are the principles behind it. Please, when it comes to depreciation of both individual items and buildings, get an accountant to do the number crunching.

....

Example

Let's go back to our example from chapter 4, in which the investor was negatively geared, 'losing' $7500 a year.

	Income	Expenses	
Rent	$18 200		
Agent's fees (8%)		$1 456	
Insurance		$700	
Rates		$700	
Maintenance		$1 000	
Subtotal	**$18 200**	**$3 856**	
Interest ($315 000 at 7%)		$22 050	
Total	**$18 200**	**$25 906**	
Total loss	**$18 200**	**– $25 906**	**= $7706**

So, our investor is down $7706 a year before depreciation is included. Let's now add some depreciation. Let's now

Example *(cont'd)*

do the numbers for both an average income earner and a high-income earner.

	31.5% tax rate	46.5% tax rate
Net loss	$7706.00	$7706.00
Tax deduction ($7706)	−$2427.39	−$3583.29
Net loss subtotal	$5278.61	$4122.71
Depreciable items ($742)	−$233.73	−$345.03
Net loss subtotal	$5044.88	$3777.68
Building depreciation ($3250)	−$1023.75	−$1511.25
Net loss total	$4021.13	$2266.43

This shows that two investors who had technically lost $7706 a year on their investment properties have had their net losses substantially narrowed through the twin effects of depreciation (for fixtures and fittings and bricks and mortar) and negative gearing. The high-income earner is now wearing a loss of just more than $2266.43 a year (about $43.59 a week), while our average income earner is slightly more than $4021.13 a year (or about $77.33 a week). This compares to each investor losing $7706, or $148.19 a week, prior to the tax benefits being applied.

Remember, however, we don't know your specific situation. This chapter, as it relates to tax, is general in nature. Changes to tax law occur regularly. If you are considering buying, or have bought, investment property, employ an accountant to advise you on tax and depreciation matters.

Chapter 10

Building a property portfolio

In this chapter we will cover the following:

▲ Setting yourself some goals

▲ Using your equity to build a portfolio

▲ Property values grow in fits and spurts

▲ Time to build a portfolio

▲ Two million dollars in debt!

▲ Ownership structure — give yourself some options

▲ Turning a negatively geared property into a positively geared one.

As financially rewarding as owning an investment property can be, sadly, just the one property probably won't make you rich.

Given enough time for the mortgage to be paid off or the rent to rise high enough, one investment property might make you very 'comfortable', allowing you to lead a lifestyle you never thought you would, but it won't make you really wealthy.

Plus, it's a bit of an exaggeration to call one property a 'portfolio', isn't it?

And while there's a lot to learn before stepping out and buying your first investment property, the good news is that you don't really have to relearn it for the second (and subsequent) purchases.

Setting yourself some goals

Clearly, by deciding to read this book, you are serious enough about property investment to want to do something about it.

But if you haven't already done so, you should ask yourself a few questions about what you want to gain out of being a property investor. What are you hoping to achieve by investing in property? Is it to make yourself (or yourselves) a little more comfortable in retirement? A lot more comfortable? Or seriously loaded?

Do you have enough patience to build a portfolio? Property investment is, largely, a long-term investment. Unless you're aiming to do a renovation to sell for a profit (see chapter 11), you should have a minimum period of 5 to 7 years in mind, because property is a cyclical asset and there can be periods of several years where there is no growth or property actually falls in value. If you're heading into property investment for a single property and a modest income, then investment over five years would be considered the minimum. However, if you're planning on becoming seriously wealthy through property, you should expect to be working on your property plan for an absolute minimum of 10, but more like 20, years.

There's little point investing in anything without a plan. Too many people just go out and buy one investment property, or shares in one company, and end up owning that asset without really knowing why they bought it in the first place (apart from a hope that they will make some money out of it): yes, they bought it for an investment; yes, it might have produced a nice income in rent or dividends; and yes, they did it because they believed that investing was the right thing to do for their future; but some people don't quite grasp why it was a good idea in the first place.

As we said in chapter 1, this book is as much a 'why to' invest in property as it is a 'how to' invest in property. Many people who do well from an investment sell quickly to lock in a (usually small) profit because they're not prepared to see out the proper life of an investment, where compound interest or investment returns act to create serious wealth. They don't necessarily grasp the longer term equation — if they made thousands of dollars over a few years from an investment, then they could make many times that amount over 10 years, 20 years, or a lifetime.

So set yourself some goals. If you would really like to build a property portfolio, then you should have some idea of what you're seeking to do. Do you want enough to supplement your income in later years? If so, perhaps two or three properties, once the mortgage is paid off, will do. Or do you want to have a rent roll that will completely replace the income from your daily employment and more? In that case you may need four, five, six, or more, properties.

Using your equity to build a portfolio

As discussed in chapter 2, your home should be the cornerstone investment of your move into property investment. If you bought your home five years ago or more, it's likely that you will have built up some equity by now. This will usually have been achieved by both paying off some of the loan and an increase in the value of the property itself.

The equity in your home — remember, a home is different to an investment — is why the bank will lend you the money for an investment property. It gives the bank security. Given enough equity as security in a home, banks will usually lend up to 110 per cent or more for residential investment property.

This means that if the house you want to buy as an investment is valued at $280 000, most banks will be confident enough to lend you the full amount, plus the other expenses involved in buying the property. (As previously discussed, these other costs include stamp duty, plus other state government charges, conveyancing costs, LMI and settlement costs.) This could mean the loan for a $280 000 property could come in at nearly $308 000 (depending on which state the purchase is made in).

Property values grow in fits and spurts

Houses don't uniformly grow in value — that would make investing just too easy and eliminate the risk! While property delivers an average total return of about 10 to 12 per cent over the years (including capital growth and the rental income), it does not grow by a set amount annually. In some years property will increase by as much as 25 per cent, while in other years it will fall in value.

In the past two decades, Australian property prices have experienced two big cycles. In the late 1980s, property prices nearly doubled in about two years following the 1987 stock-market crash; however, as with all booms, it was followed by a bust. Between 1990 and 1992, Sydney's property prices fell in actual terms by as much as 25 per cent and Melbourne's prices fell 10 per cent, while the falls across the rest of the state capitals were not as pronounced. The bust would have been even worse if calculated in real terms (where inflation is included).

For years afterwards, there was no growth. Australia's property market was essentially flat until about 1996. Then, between 1996 and 2003, first Melbourne and then Sydney property prices rose significantly. They didn't double in two years like they did in the late 1980s, but they did increase by about 70 to 90 per cent during that period.

Since the end of 2003, prices have fallen again in the two largest capitals. Meanwhile, in Brisbane, Adelaide, Canberra and Hobart, prices have 'flattened' or 'cooled', meaning that they have either risen slowly, are fairly steady or have been slowly falling. However, in Perth and Darwin, prices were still going gangbusters in mid 2006, thanks largely to the global resources boom, which is fuelling demand and boosting pay packets for staff in mining and related industries.

Property prices are affected by many things. They may grow at 20 per cent (potentially more) for a year or they may even exhibit similar sorts of growth for two, three or four years. Then again, they may do nothing, or very little, for extended periods as well.

Property prices can grow in fits and spurts, followed by nothing. While you can never expect a property to grow uniformly in value, at least, with very rare exceptions, you can expect it to grow over time.

Time to build a portfolio

If you have set yourself a goal in property investment and are trying to move steadily towards it, you have to be aware that it may take a little longer than you anticipated if the market flattens out. Equally, a couple of good years could mean you get to where you wanted faster than you had anticipated.

Generally, building a portfolio takes time, no matter what some property spruikers tell you at their seminars. You should not expect to become an overnight millionaire from property. But it is quite reasonable to expect that, by using a buy and hold strategy where you keep on buying a house every few years as property prices increase, you will have built a sizeable portfolio in 10 to 20 years. The rents from the properties (plus the tax benefits) not only mean the properties often pay for themselves, but also that they will even provide you with a passive income. Plus, you will have developed a portfolio that contains significant equity.

It is possible that, over time, a couple (or a single person) with average incomes can build a portfolio of properties worth several million dollars. That portfolio will come with plenty of debt too — but don't let that scare you. Don't forget that you will have the tenant and the tax man helping you out.

To demonstrate how a property portfolio can be beneficial in the long run, let's use what is (hopefully) a typical scenario for many people reading this book. Our couple is Michael, 45, and Lisa, 44.

....

Case study—Michael and Lisa

Michael and Lisa bought a home seven years ago. They paid $250000 for it and it's now worth $370000. They took out a loan of $220000 for the house, which has been paid down to about $160000, giving them equity of $210000. They have decided to build a portfolio of five properties, which they believe should give them enough income on which to potentially retire after the properties' debts have been paid off.

Year 1

They have found an investment property for $300000 that fits the criteria they have drawn up—a three-year-old house (which will give them some building depreciation benefits) about 10 kilometres from the city. Because they still have debt on their home, they opt to borrow everything they can for the investment property and make the loan interest only. That has left Michael and Lisa with a new loan of approximately $318000.

They now have two houses, worth a combined $670000, with total debt of $478000.

Historically, house prices have grown by about 10 per cent a year over many decades. However, we will factor in growth of 8 per cent for two reasons. The first reason is that it's better to be a little conservative, so that we don't over-inflate property prices. The second reason is that the historical growth rate of 10 per cent accommodates the effects of periods of much higher inflation than we have recently experienced in Australia.

Year 3

Two years after Michael and Lisa bought their investment property, the value of both of their properties (home and investment) has grown to approximately $781000 (their home is worth $431000 and the investment property is worth $350000). The debt on both properties has marginally fallen to $455000.

They now have combined equity in both properties of about $311000—enough for their financial institution to be confident in lending to them again.

They decide to buy another investment property. The property will be similar to the last one they bought, but in a different area (perhaps interstate) to diversify their risk. The new property is worth $350000 and the new loan is for $371000. Now, their three properties are worth a total of $1.131 million, and they have total debt of $826000

Year 5

Their three properties are now worth $1.319 million and their debt has fallen to about $812000. They now have equity of $507000—ensuring that the bank is comfortable enough to lend to them again.

If Michael and Lisa continue to buy a house every two years (years 1, 3, 5, 7 and 9), by year 11 they will have:

- five investment properties inside of 10 years

- investment properties valued at approximately $3.22 million (about $4.02 million if we include their home)

- investment debt of about $2.17 million (plus another $80000 for home)

Case study *(cont'd)*

- net equity in the investment properties of around $1.05 million ($1.77 million if their home is included)

- an investment-property asset base that should now increase in value by more than $250000 in the next year

- the rent from five properties, an income stream that, over time, should rise with inflation and help reduce the debt.

In about a decade, Michael and Lisa (with the help of tenants and the tax man) have built themselves a significant asset base. They could keep going if they wanted to—many investors do. They could also choose to sell one of the properties to pay down the debt faster on the remaining four or they could choose to continue holding all five properties, not purchase any more, and simply pay down the debt over time as planned. Planning is the key. All investors should have a plan, as discussed earlier.

Two million dollars in debt!

Most people will gasp when they realise the debt. The above situation means that Michael and Lisa will owe their bank more than $2 million.

Two million dollars!

Fear of debt is something that many people learn from their parents. Most of us were taught by our elders that we should get a job, buy a home, pay it off and then later in life put any income that we're not using towards the mortgage to invest.

However, the reality is that the 'average' investor can't buy property with savings alone. And taxwise, it doesn't make sense to pay cash for a property. This is particularly relevant if you've also got a mortgage on your home, because while the debt on your home (or 'principal place of residence') is not tax deductible, debt for investment is.

Also, don't forget that you are not going to be faced with that whole $2.2 million debt in one go. The debt has developed over a decade as your total asset base and income (through rent) grew. In other words, your income is growing over time from the rent being charged for the properties and your debt is backed by assets worth approximately $4 million.

Start off small. Buy one investment property and make that a success. After a few years (and some capital growth), you will have seen how rental income and the tax man can be used to your advantage, perhaps making you feel comfortable enough to take on more property investment debt.

Ownership structure — give yourself some options

If your intention is to build a property portfolio, and you are not a solo investor, then you should put some thought into your portfolio's ownership structure.

As discussed in chapter 4, there are many options for property investment that are relevant to whether a property is positively or negatively geared. While there is often nothing wrong with an investment property being bought in two names (for example, a husband and a wife), there will be some situations where it may be more appropriate for the holding to be in the name of just one individual. For example, for tax reasons, couples might wish to consider putting positively geared properties in the name of the lower income-earning partner. The advantage of this would be that less tax would be paid on that partner's net income. On the other hand, negatively geared properties in the name of the higher earning partner could be more beneficial.

This is an important topic for investor couples to discuss. It's wise to seek the advice of both tax and legal professionals because they'll be able to give you advice on what would be most beneficial in your particular situation.

When it comes to building a portfolio of properties, investors should give some thought to different sorts of ownership within the portfolio. The ownership options you choose will not only be relevant to ongoing gearing and tax purposes, but they will also make a difference when it comes to selling a property.

Michael and Lisa, for example, could buy all their properties in joint names if they wished, but if one of them was on a considerably higher tax rate at the time they decided to sell the property, then they would be in a situation where one paid a high rate of tax on their portion of the sale and the other paid a much lower rate of tax.

However, let's say that out of their five properties three were bought jointly and two were held individually — one in Michael's name and one in Lisa's name.

That would give three ownership structures (joint ownership for three properties, individual ownership under Michael's name and individual ownership under Lisa's name) and a range of options if they ever decided to sell a property. If, for example, Lisa was to retire earlier than Michael (say, when she is 60, in about year 18 of their portfolio development) and the decision was made to sell a property to reduce some debt, then it might make sense to sell the property in her name from a tax perspective after she had retired, thereby minimising the CGT to be paid. Likewise, if Michael was to retire first it could be advantageous to sell the property that is in his name.

Taking advantage of different ownership structures when purchasing a property could save some money on tax down the track, because, in some states, there is limited ability to transfer ownership between spouses without incurring new stamp duty. Although, it might not be beneficial to change the ownership structure because it could lead to a CGT event, which could leave you with an up-front tax bill. Always seek expert advice on this matter.

Turning a negatively geared property into a positively geared one

At the time of writing, the majority of houses (but not necessarily flats or units) purchased in capital cities will be negatively geared if the full purchase price, plus costs, is borrowed. This is because house prices have seen a period of sustained growth in the late 1990s and early 2000s that was not matched by increasing rents.

However, remember that, over time—sometimes it takes many years—rents do rise, eventually turning a negatively geared property into a positively geared one.

Landlords don't just have to wait for rents to rise with inflation; they can be proactive and do things to increase the rent that the property receives. Sometimes it may be slapping on a fresh coat of paint, or adding features like an air conditioner or a dishwasher, that adds another $5 or $10 to the weekly rent. If a dishwasher costs $600, but allows you to get an extra $10 a week in rent, it will pay for itself in a little longer than one year and will continue to add rental value for years—and it's also a depreciable asset.

If you have built a portfolio, like Michael and Lisa, of about five properties over a decade, then you may well find some of the earlier properties have evolved from being negatively geared to being positively geared. The income from the earlier properties would then help offset the costs of the negatively geared properties that were bought later.

Chapter 11

Renovating for profit

In this chapter we will cover the following:

▲ Assessing the potential

▲ Location

▲ Building type

▲ Strata titles versus freehold titles

▲ Cosmetic renovations versus structural renovations

▲ Big-ticket renovation items

▲ Gardens

▲ Overcapitalising

▲ Getting 'the look'

▲ Budgets and finance.

Assessing the potential

Before you launch into a renovation or start prowling the market looking for that undervalued 'renovator's delight', do your homework. Yes, that old advice again!

Whenever you make a decision about your investment properties, you must be able to justify it in terms of your budget and long-term investment plan — which goes for renovating too.

Buying to renovate

There is no point in cruising the inner-city suburbs or checking out <realestate.com.au> for run-down terrace homes and workers' cottages if your long-term portfolio aim is to target the family market or if you only have a small budget. If there's one broad rule about buying in the inner city, it's that it's expensive and more likely to be tenanted by young single people than families.

No matter how much of a bargain you think the property is, if it doesn't fit in with your long-term portfolio, or meet your risk tolerance and budget constraints, forget it. Move on and look for something else.

....

Tried and true

Renovation tax treatment

Be aware that the costs of most renovation work, including small jobs such as painting and decorating, polishing floorboards, replacing the front fence and even repairing the roof, are not usually tax deductible in your first year of ownership.

These items usually have to be treated as a capital expense, which means they are added to the total cost base of the property and can't be claimed against income in that year, but instead, will have to be depreciated over many years.

Check with your tax adviser because, usually, the ATO doesn't allow even 'repair and maintenance' costs for a recently purchased property. The reason for this is that you can generally only claim repair or maintenance costs for damage or deterioration that has occurred to the property while you have been earning an income from it.

In other words, since you have only just purchased the property, any existing damage or deterioration could not have occurred during the time you were earning an income from it.

This even applies if you buy at a discount. Some buyers reduce the purchase price by the estimated cost of fixing certain defects. The ATO, however, will not usually allow the cost of these repairs to be deducted.

See chapter 9 for more on tax issues.

Renovating existing property

If you are planning to renovate a property you already own, you need to ask yourself if the renovation fits your overall, long-term plan. Whether you buy to renovate or to fix up something you already own, the big question will be, 'Is it going to make financial sense?' Will spending the money on a renovation give you a greater return, either through earning more rent or through receiving a higher price when you sell?

To assess whether you should renovate, calculate the rent you will earn if the property isn't renovated and compare it with what you think you will earn after it has been fixed up. The same goes for the resale price — compare what you think you will get by selling it 'as is' with the price you think you'll receive if you sell it after a renovation.

In most cases, you will earn more after a renovation; although, in a tough rental market, when vacancies are high, this may not happen. However, if you do renovate, it may mean you will attract a tenant when the renovations are finished — which is better than having an empty, unrenovated property.

Also, the higher rent or resale price may still neither be worth the effort, nor worth the extra interest payments you will have to make on a loan used to fund the renovation.

A good tip for helping you to decide what to spend on improvements is to compare other properties — use the internet to see the rental prices that other properties are going for. A couple of hours spent browsing on <realestate.com.au> should give you enough information for you to see if properties with new kitchens or two bathrooms, for example, are earning significantly higher rent than those without.

Once you have worked out the basic financial benefit (for example, the rent should go up from $230 per week to $280 per week, or the estimated resale price may rise by about $100 000 or more), you will still have to decide if the carrying cost of that extra interest payment is worthwhile. In economic terms this is known as 'opportunity cost' — knowing how you could use that $50 000 renovation money if you didn't put it into fixing your property.

You need to ask yourself some questions. Would you be better off using this money as the deposit for another property? Would you be better off splitting the $50 000 across two properties and upgrading only part of each? Would you be better off selling this property and buying one already renovated? If you don't expect to earn extra rent immediately from the renovation, do you have the cash flow to keep up the interest repayments on the extra $50 000 during the renovation and while you wait to sell it?

So, when you are assessing the potential, you cannot just assume that the property will provide you with a higher return. You will have to consider any lost opportunity from using the money for a different purpose, as well as the extra hassle of renovating and the possible months of downtime during a renovation when the property could be empty or earning less income (if the tenants are given a rental discount in lieu of the disruption).

Location

Location, location, location. Yes, it's importance to real estate never changes. It's a time-honoured rule of property ownership and useful to keep in mind when you are renovating.

You can always fix the house (well, almost always) but you can't always fix the location. So make sure you are in the right location before planning a renovation — remembering that certain suburbs and areas have a particular market.

Typically, it is best to 'renovate to your market', which means keeping it to the scale and proportion of neighbouring properties and ensuring it meets tenant expectations in that particular market.

In other words, you can't turn a standard 1970s cream-brick suburban home into an inner-city warehouse — so don't even try. Young families will not necessarily pay more for a room dedicated to a spa bath or gymnasium set-up. Trendy singles or empty nesters as tenants may, however, be willing to dish out an extra $100 a week to have a home-gym. It's all a matter of knowing your market — meaning your prospective tenants and your resale market, when it comes time to sell.

If you do decide to go against the market and do something extraordinary with your renovations, make sure you are aware of the risk. If tenants who are attracted to this type of renovation are few and far between in your area, then you may have to add an extra month to the typical vacancy period to draw interest. Likewise, if buyers for this type of renovation are scarce, then you may have to wait longer to find someone willing to purchase the property or lower your sale price expectations due to a lack of competition for your property.

Whether you are renovating for a higher resale value or higher rents, it is a risk that you have to weigh up as part of your renovation assessment.

Building type

Certain building types are easier to renovate than others. Freestanding weatherboard houses, for example, are probably the easiest buildings to renovate. Weatherboards are relatively easy to cut out to add doorways or windows, as well as to add additional rooms, compared with brickwork or concrete slab construction. Freestanding houses are also easier to renovate because there is room to access all sides of the property and no adjoining structures to consider.

However, all building types can be renovated. Of course, because of structural issues, special permission will usually be required at the planning and permit stage before tackling a semi-detached terrace home, townhouse or apartment. This generally means more cost, due to initial engineering and surveying requirements, specialised construction techniques or from the process just taking longer than it would for a straightforward, freestanding home.

Strata titles versus freehold titles

Probably the biggest issue with renovating is getting all the approvals in place. As well as soil, structural, planning and building permits, if you own a strata title property or company share title, you will also need to get approval from your body corporate or company board.

In many cases, body corporate rules will control what you can and can't do within your property and that may include renovating or even just rewiring or upgrading bathroom or kitchen plumbing.

Depending on its rules, the mighty body corporate can prevent you renovating if the remodelling is going to alter the external appearance, disrupt building services or even just annoy other owners or tenants.

In many of the newer high-rise apartments, even the colour of the window blinds is regulated to ensure that the property gives a uniform appearance from the street. So it pays to double-check the body corporate rules or get a legal opinion before buying a strata title property with a view to renovation.

Cosmetic renovations versus structural renovations

There is a huge time and cost difference between being able to cosmetically improve a property and undertaking a structural renovation. In most cases, cosmetic improvements are relatively quick and cheap; however, structural changes require specialised tradespeople, a lot of time and usually a lot of money. Types of cosmetic and structural renovations are listed in table 11.1.

Table 11.1: types of cosmetic renovations and structural renovations

Cosmetic renovations	Structural renovations
• polishing floor boards	• new roof
• re-tiling walls or floors	• adding a room
• painting	• damp proofing
• carpeting	• demolishing walls
• new stove	• rewiring
• new kitchen cupboards	• re-plumbing
• built-in wardrobes	• creating new doorways or windows
• replacing bath, sink, toilet or shower	• underpinning or new stumps

Table 11.1 *(cont'd)*: types of cosmetic renovations and structural renovations

Cosmetic renovations	Structural renovations
• replacing windows • replanting the garden • opening up old fireplaces • re-plastering • general repairs and presentation • minor floor-plan changes • decorating.	• repairing or moving brickwork or supporting walls • structural dry rot or white-ant damage.

The decision-making process behind making structural improvements requires a cost–benefit analysis. In other words, will the cost give you an equal or greater benefit?

If you can stick to cosmetic improvements, it will be cheaper and the cost–benefit will probably be greater; however, skimping on a major structural problem means you carry an ongoing risk within your portfolio.

If you replace the roof instead of repairing it, what will the difference be? The biggest difference will be the immediate cost (for example, $10 000 to replace the roof compared with $2500 to repair it).

How long will the new roof be trouble-free compared with the repaired roof? If you are selling, perhaps you think this won't matter; but astute buyers will always look for roof problems and signs of repair. If they see the roof is brand new, then they can pretty much give the roof a big tick of approval.

If you are planning to rent out the property, the question is the same. You don't want to have the tenants complaining (and rightly so) every time the roof leaks. So you might have to factor in ongoing repairs and possibly disgruntled tenants.

Big-ticket renovation items

Big-ticket items are the renovation budget blowers — the things that eat up your money, sometimes with very little to show on the outside and little obvious rental or capital improvement. Big-ticket renovation items can include:

▲ wiring

▲ plumbing

▲ bathrooms

▲ kitchens

▲ foundations

▲ roofing.

Wiring and plumbing

If you have a house with dodgy wiring or plumbing, you may as well just start signing the cheques, because fix-up jobs are not an option in either case. Wiring and plumbing are invisible to the tenant's eye, and to the eye of some future buyers, but they are probably the two most important items that you can't skimp on.

Dodgy wiring can cause death, fires and equipment faults, and it is a hidden peril in many older properties. Dubious plumbing, while not fatal, can cause constant problems for tenants (and therefore owners) and serious degenerative structural damage to your property, such as the effects of rising damp. In almost every case, plumbing and wiring need to be fixed properly and kept in tip-top condition.

Bathrooms and kitchens

Bathrooms and kitchens are two rooms into which you can pour money and never stop. Fashion and design features abound in these two zones of the home and they are the most difficult areas to keep up to date.

Women, in particular, are harsh critics of kitchens and bathrooms and if you are trying to appeal to a female market then these areas need to meet certain standards. This does not necessarily mean swanky cooktops and four-head shower cubicles, but it does mean clean, serviceable areas, appliances in good working order and a degree of effort in the presentation.

Bathroom fittings and kitchen appliances can cost anywhere from a few hundred dollars to many thousands of dollars, but they are not necessarily what is required to improve a kitchen or bathroom. Renovating these two zones of the house requires careful thought and planning, not necessarily a big budget — some minor cosmetic changes could be all that is required to make a property more attractive to tenants. For example:

▲   A shower head installed over a bath — even though not desirable to all tenants — is still better than a property with just a bath and no option to have a shower. Installing a separate shower cubicle will win out in most cases.

▲   A separate toilet, or additional toilet, will be a good rental feature in a share house and give you an edge over another house without this feature.

▲   A larger space in the kitchen for a fridge can mean the difference between getting a tenant or not, especially if the tenant already has a double-fronted fridge and no hope of squeezing it into a small alcove.

▲   A dishwasher is usually a big drawcard for most tenants.

▲   Designer taps do not usually influence a tenant's decision-making process when choosing a property; however, new benchtops and cupboard fronts may make a difference.

Foundations

Foundations are another Pandora's box of costs when it comes to your renovation budget. If you are buying a property with a plan to renovate it, the foundations should always be checked as part of your pre-purchase homework. Any major defects will show up during this inspection and you can price your offer for the property accordingly.

If you are renovating a property you already own and experience problems with the foundations or structure, then you have two options. The first is to repair it—restump, underpin or fix the brickwork—and the second option is to sell and move on (of course, with the sale option comes the potential discount in price for the canny buyers who undertake a pre-purchase building inspection report). So it all comes back to the cost–benefit decision. Will the cost of the repair or renovation be worth it to you? Will you make more money from it? If so, how much more? What could you do with that money otherwise?

Australia has had several long periods of drought and will probably continue to do so. In many areas, this means substantial movement in house structure as the water table falls and the soil around our homes and apartment buildings dries out completely—evidence of cracking is not necessarily an indicator of major foundation or structural problems. In many cases, rehydrating the soil can cause cracks to close up again; but it is a highly technical area of expertise and the kind of analysis that is always best done by an expert.

Roofing

The style, height and material of the roof will dictate how expensive it is to fix or replace. For example, the more ridge lines and angles the roof has — the dearer it will be. A two-storey house will usually require scaffolding (a big expense), while material costs can range from secondhand corrugated iron to laminated glass, with price tags to match.

Typically, slate is the most expensive of the traditional roofing materials, not only because it is expensive to manufacture into tiles, but also because tradespeople capable of repairing or replacing tile roofs are increasingly hard to find.

Corrugated iron is practically an Australian icon — and the most popular roofing material in the country. It has progressed from our settlers' tin-roofed shacks to becoming almost a designer item for both contemporary and period architecture. Its benefits include being relatively easy and light for tradesmen (and DIY renovators) to work with, and the sheets can be lifted and replaced without disturbing other parts of the roof.

Terracotta and cement tiles also have their advantages. They, too, can usually be lifted individually and replaced without too much expense or difficulty — although this is probably beyond the skill of most DIY renovators.

Whatever the material or style of roof, the most important thing to ensure is that it's doing its job properly — by keeping out the weather!

Handy tip

While a slumped or wonky ridgeline should be obvious from looking at the roof from across the street, an internal inspection — yes, up there inside the manhole — is still vital for any pre-purchase assessment. Although some people may be tempted to do this themselves, some defects (or potential defects), such as rafter strength, insect infestation or long-term water damage, are not always obvious to an untrained eye. A professional opinion is the best way to go in most cases.

Gardens

In the property development game, there is a general rule of thumb that you spend at least 10 per cent of your budget on the garden. Although this mainly applies to developers and new housing estates, it can also be applied to investment properties.

A garden is a major selling point and drawcard for two reasons. The front garden adds to the property's street appeal, is a big drawcard for tenants and future owners, and the back garden adds to the property's lifestyle appeal.

The same applies to balconies, courtyards and shared common areas at apartment blocks. A unit with a balcony, even a small balcony, offers the tenants or purchasers the potential for alfresco dining, the chance to grow their own herbs, a place to sit in the sun or just a temporary escape from the people inside.

A courtyard offers that little bit more — somewhere tenants can actually cultivate a small garden, set up a clothes line, entertain guests or allow a pet safe outdoor access.

If you have an opportunity to create a balcony or courtyard as part of your renovation, go for it. For relatively little expense you will be creating an additional room and the promise of a better lifestyle — features both tenants and buyers will appreciate.

As far as what type of garden or landscaping you decide on, look to your neighbours. Take a stroll around the neighbourhood and make a note of all the plants that are thriving. These plants are obviously suited to the area and climate, and by buying them for your property you will spend less money on dying plants and less time nurturing plants that aren't suited to the soil and conditions.

A key ambition to have in mind with every garden, no matter what style — whether formal, cottage, rambling or woodland — is to make it low maintenance. The less maintenance you or your tenants have to do, the happier everyone is going to be.

Mass planting of a single species or only two or three species always makes a statement and looks neat and tidy. Mass planting of drought-tolerant plants means they will look good and also virtually look after themselves. This style of planting can be used in courtyards, suburban yards and even farm blocks.

Also, because people have to pay for water, drought-tolerant plants will also be an added attraction for potential tenants and buyers.

Tried and true

Hard landscaping—such as concrete, brickwork, paving and terraces—is the most expensive item in the garden.

Gravel paths, feature pavers or stepping stones set in grass or ground cover is an excellent and far cheaper alternative for pathways.

Overcapitalising

'Overcapitalising' basically means spending too much money on your renovation and not getting enough back in return. This can result from not generating a big enough increase in rent, or from not obtaining a high enough resale price.

Larger renovations such as adding a second bathroom, extra bedroom, second storey or double garage need to be weighed against the financial outlay and the proposed financial benefit. As a rule of thumb, the more upmarket the area, the more upmarket the home (and the tenant)—meaning both a higher rent and eventual sale price.

However, a modest home in an upmarket area is also going to be in high demand—if not in higher demand—simply because it is a rarity and will allow someone to live in that area at a relatively discounted price.

A four-bedroom house in one of the most expensive locations in your city or region will earn more rent if it has two bathrooms, two living areas, separate dining space and a double garage.

However, because it is probably typical housing stock and relatively common, most rents and purchase prices for this type of house will be roughly the same.

A more modest three-bedroom home with only one bathroom and combined living and dining spaces will potentially have a greater pool of tenants because at $70- or $80-a-week cheaper, it will be affordable for a greater range of people who also want to live in the expensive location. With potential resale price in mind, it will also have a greater pool of potential buyers because it offers a discounted entry price for a highly regarded area. So, in other words, 'under capitalising' can be a deliberate strategy too.

Back to 'overcapitalising' and that old cost–benefit decision again. You need to ask yourself if it is worth spending the money. A reasonable way to help make this decision is to find out how much a similar example of your property — after it is renovated — has sold for recently in your area. If a renovated two-bedroom, semi-detached house with an off-street car park and a courtyard sold for, say, $310 000, then you need to decide how much you are willing to spend to create a matching off-street car park and courtyard to achieve the same price.

If your property is valued at $290 000 and your quotes come in at about $20 000 for the car space and courtyard — are the renovations worth it when the house down the road sold for only $310 000, merely breaking even with your outlay? If the house down the road sold for $315 000 and you can match it by spending a total of $310 000, is a potential $5000 profit worth the risk?

You may still be better off selling your property 'as is' and marketing it as having the potential for an off-street car park and courtyard, which will let buyers put their own value on that potential.

The cost–benefit decision also applies to adding these features in order to earn higher rent. If an off-street car park earns an additional $20 a week in rent, will this cover the interest costs of borrowing the additional $20 000 to create it?

The key to avoiding overcapitalising is to make sure your purchase price plus your renovation cost is less than recent sale prices of similar properties.

Getting 'the look'

Notions of what is fashionable extends to furniture design, paint colour, carpet, architecture, town planning and even tap design, and they all rely on one thing — change.

Changing fashions mean that you may decide to spend your money on keeping up with the latest trends. Whether you are updating colours, replanting gardens, redesigning living areas or buying property in new areas — you name it — the fashion-makers will change it.

However, as far as getting 'the look' from your renovation, there are some tried and true tips to keep you on the right track and prevent too much money being swallowed up by the 'fashion' industry.

Floors

You often can't beat wooden floorboards. They've been around as long as most civilisations — and new protective coatings developed during the past 60 years or so have made them even more practical. So be they polished, waxed or varnished, floorboards and parquetry are sensible and attractive.

If you are deciding between flooring options — go wooden. Most people now know the benefits of wooden floors. They are easy to clean, hard-wearing, and when they do wear, they still look good. They can be dressed up easily and made to look fashionable by adding rugs or carpet squares, and they are a neutral background for other decorations and furnishings.

There are also various wooden-floor options for overlaying concrete slabs and some include substantial insulation to help deaden noise if the property is multi-level.

If carpet is your best option, try for a 100 per cent wool or as close to this as your budget will allow. It is longer wearing, often the dye colours are more intense and it resists stains and scorches.

Wall colour

Developers and real estate players will usually advise you to keep your background wall colours neutral and classic — these colours are usually warm and versatile. What this usually means is an off-white or a soft beige that almost no-one will find offensive. One of the main aims in presentation is to avoid someone seeing your property and saying, 'There's no way I can live with that black feature wall or those orange tiles.' You don't want to give potential tenants or buyers a reason to discount the property.

However, neutral colours do not necessarily mean boring. You can enliven otherwise dreary wall colours by strategically placing bright or colourful items near them. Polished wood floors and neutral wall colours can easily be set off with a bold splash of colour on kitchen cupboard doors, or with colourful curtains or blinds. Better still, a wall-hanging or piece of art that adds vibrancy but is not a fixture means the potential buyer does not have to share your taste but can still appreciate the property's potential.

If you are trying to rent out or sell your property, the key to getting 'the look' is to make as many people as possible think that they could easily live there. The aim is to make them feel that all they have to do is move in their furniture and relax.

It is also important to know your target market. If you have a one-bedroom unit in a typical suburban apartment block, then keeping colours uniform throughout the property will give an impression of more space, because the rooms will blend into each other with no obvious delineation between areas. Also, removing the odd internal door (although it's not a good idea to remove the bathroom door) can help create a feeling of open-plan living, especially between the kitchen and a living area, or even a living area and a bedroom.

If you have a three-bedroom house in the outer suburbs or in a regional area, then the chances are your tenants (and future buyers) will be a family. In this case, practical surfaces may be more important—washable paints and a wall colour that does not show marks is often a priority for this market.

When it comes to the overall presentation of your property, clean and fresh usually wins the day. Freshening up paintwork on doors and skirting trims, and ensuring that ceilings are a crisp white and that the property is clean during inspections will help make your property a winner.

Budgets and finance

You may have to fund your renovation from more borrowed money. It is usually a relatively easy step that, for many people, will involve simply redrawing or extending an existing mortgage. However, if you have had your mortgage for several years, but are not sure if you've built up any additional equity, you should have your property revalued.

As a general rule, the best way to finance a renovation is through the existing mortgage on your investment property. It means the additional funds are already lodged against your investment loan, which makes it clear to the ATO that the funds (and the interest) are related to your investment asset.

Setting a budget for your renovation is the hard part. Once again, the cost–benefit decision comes into play. The first step involves making a list of everything you want to do. Then you need to get a price or quote for these modifications, which is easier said than done.

Comparing quotes

Your specifications are what the builder will use to quote on. They should have as much detail and description as possible to enable you to have everything you want the way you want it and, more importantly, so that you have quotes you can properly compare.

As a general guide, three quotes will usually give you a high, low and middle price. Don't be tempted to just take the middle price or the low price. Once you have the written quotes in front of you, carefully go through each quote and ensure they have included your specifications. Make sure the following details are listed in your quotes:

▲ solid plastering (if it is an older or period home) — not plasterboard or just 'replastering'

▲ undercoat and two top coats of paint to all exterior surfaces — not just 'paint'

▲ brand names and item numbers of particular fittings

▲ completion timetable — with no fixed end date, the renovation can drag on.

Once you have compared quotes, talk to each builder and check that they all have included your requirements. A heavily discounted price could mean that a major item has been overlooked but that the rest of the quote still provides better value than the others.

It is only after you are sure about the total cost of the renovation that you can crunch the numbers on your calculator and decide if you really can afford it. If you find that you are in danger of overcapitalising, then you may have to take off some alterations or reduce the size of the project. If you still won't be earning enough of a return — either in rent or future capital gain — don't renovate.

Sometimes it is better to accept the rental income or capital gain from your property, as it stands, rather than renovating it and making a loss.

Chapter 12

Holiday homes

In this chapter we will cover the following:

▲ The dream

▲ The reality

▲ Judging the potential

▲ Coastal property

▲ Rural property

▲ Golf course property

▲ Serviced apartments

▲ Tax considerations

▲ Financing.

The dream

Summer is usually the peak time for holiday-home purchases, or at least the peak holiday-home browsing period, as people flock to coastal and regional areas for their annual holidays.

It's common to see people outside coastal real estate offices cruising the window displays, looking at properties for sale. When they get home they may log on to their laptops and PCs to surf the market. (In fact, as someone interested in real estate, you might have done this yourself.)

If you are one of the growing number of people who have rented a home for a holiday period and forked out a huge sum for the privilege, it's easy to think there might be a cheaper way to have a holiday. And if you are a regular to that holiday destination, you will no doubt have noticed the rapid rise in accommodation prices in the past few years.

People usually think to themselves, 'Wouldn't it be great if we could have our own holiday home? Then we could come here whenever we liked and, when we're not using it, we could rent it out and earn some extra money. Perhaps, we could even save some tax through negatively gearing it!' It sounds like the best of both worlds — a holiday house 'on call', with tenants and the tax man to help you pay it off! Realising this dream is not as simple as it sounds.

The reality

Holiday homes and investment properties should be kept completely separate. If you are using a property as a holiday home, chances are it is not being marketed to its full potential or rented in a way that earns its maximum income. What you will end up with is a holiday home that you might not be able to use when you want to and an investment property that is not earning enough of a return to justify having your money tied up.

It is almost impossible to mix the two ambitions.

However, the ATO will allow investors to apportion part of their expenses from an investment property if they also use that property for private purposes. For example, if you or your family use the property for half the year and have it available for rent for the other half, then you may have a reasonable case to claim 50 per cent of the expenses against the income you earned during the time it was rented out. However, it's not quite so easy (see 'tax considerations' later in this chapter).

Generally, returns from holiday-home investment properties are lower than returns from other types of investment properties. This is often because the rental income from holiday homes can fluctuate or, if the property is permanently rented, the weekly rent is usually less than the rental income a property in a metropolitan area could earn.

Based on rental income, annual yields can be less than 2 per cent in many holiday-home markets. However, significant capital gains during the past few years have helped justify continued investment in these markets, with some areas recording price rises of more than double those of some metropolitan areas.

Judging the potential

If you are buying a holiday property for capital gain purposes, you could be on to a good thing. The trend of families, couples and singles relocating to seaside towns around the country is having a massive impact on real estate by pushing property prices to new highs.

Also likely to aid this growth is the increase of buyers in the wealthy baby-boomer market, as this demographic group seeks to secure a holiday home (or a slice of their 'future retirement market') ahead of actually retiring and relocating permanently.

During the past decade or so, the demand for coastal (sea-change), rural (tree-change) and alpine (ski-change) properties has skyrocketed.

People who already own this type of property could find themselves making significant capital gains when they sell (unless the trend reverses). They may also break even or make a positive net income from rentals, as the cost of renting these homes has also soared in the past five years.

Despite this, it's worth remembering that future growth in rents and prices may be slower. If you are just entering this market now, you will need to hold on to this type of asset for a few years longer than in the recent past to ensure you make a strong capital gain.

There may be the ongoing potential to renovate and immediately resell the property; however, often these 'renovator's delights' are being snapped up by the permanent sea-changers who, typically, plan to work part-time, do up the old cottage, and improve their lifestyle.

You may have to rely on earning an income from your holiday-market investment until a stronger capital gain makes selling the property worthwhile — or you relocate there and live in the property yourself. The tricky part will be earning a decent income from it in the interim.

Most holiday markets have a small permanent population and a huge influx of visitors and absentee owners during peak times. As an investor, that means you need to make your money in these peak periods — and you'll need enough money to tide you through the off-peak times.

Handy hint

If you earn $1500 a week during the peak holiday period for your three-bedroom property, that income is probably only sustainable for eight weeks a year—four to six weeks over the summer (or the ski season) and another two weeks at other peak times, such as at Easter or during school holidays. In this scenario, if the property is rented for the maximum eight weeks at $1500 a week, that's $12000 annual income.

However, rental income in peak periods is not a certainty. If the weather is lousy, the trend turns away from your particular location, the tenants don't turn up (leaving you with the deposit but no full rental income) or something goes wrong with the house (which means you will have to discount the rent or will not be able to rent it at all), then you can easily be caught short.

If you decide to offer the house as a permanent rental—while you hold it and wait for that juicy capital gain—then the chances are it will not earn anywhere near the rental income of a three-bedroom property in a city or regional town. It's worth remembering that wages and salaries are often significantly lower in small economies such as holiday markets, despite them having a reasonably high cost of living.

Many jobs are seasonal—in line with the tourism and peak visitor times—and casual and part-time work is common in these locations. So, although most permanent rents will work out to be about the same or slightly less than a holiday rental on an annual basis, they are also usually significantly lower than their city or suburban counterparts.

A house that could earn $1500 a week in peak season, could potentially be rented out for $200 a week on a permanent basis—leaving about $10400 in annual income. Although it is less than holiday-rental income, it is probably more reliable and may help with your cash flow throughout the year, rather than having holiday rent, which you will only receive seasonally.

Coastal property

Seaside property is probably the first thing that springs to mind when people in Australia think about the holiday-home market. It is an Australian tradition to flock to the beach as often as the weather permits. Although, even winter beaches have their attractions and properties can earn income during the off-season if they can offer an added feature such as an open fire or a view of crashing waves.

The majority of our coastal property is close to the beach, but not necessarily with a view or anything special apart from its general location in or near a seaside town.

Checklist of things to consider when choosing a beach-house investment:

☑ The distance of the property to amenities. A short stroll to the shops or nearby services will be an added bonus that holiday-makers will be prepared to pay for.

☑ Asbestos in the property. Although it is safe while undisturbed, any renovations or future upgrades may result in additional safety and handling problems, which could cost lots of money to decontaminate.

☑ Local planning regulations for special requirements or restrictions on use or future development. You may not intend to redevelop the property but your future buyers might.

☑ Local festivals and attractions. These will provide additional reasons for tourists and holiday-makers to go to your location at times outside the traditional holiday periods.

Did you know?

Coastal populations are growing at a faster rate than those in almost any other sector.

Over the past five years, coastal councils around Australia recorded growth of about 10.2 per cent (or 2 per cent compound a year).

This compares with an annual growth of 1.2 per cent across the whole of Australia. Only capital-city populations are growing at a faster rate than coastal areas.

Source: Australian Bureau of Statistics,
the National Sea Change Taskforce and Planning
Research Centre at the University of Sydney

Rural property

It's hard to imagine something more romantic and comforting than relaxing in a big country house surrounded by a wide verandah overlooking a magnificent garden. Images of a country kitchen come to mind, with its scrub-top wooden table where family and friends gather for leisurely weekend breakfasts, while lunch is held under the trees and a candle-lit dinner is set on the verandah. Dogs and kids rollicking through the garden … screeching halt! Come on, back to reality.

Yes, country properties are romantic and desirable, but they can also be one of the worst-performing property investments. The sheer size of Australia means there is an unending choice of locations and regional variations that will be competing against your property. As scarcity is a determinant of property value, it's logical that rural retreats — which are by no means scarce in a country as vast as Australia — tend to be less valuable.

Unlike seaside properties, a country house can be almost anywhere — an outback station, a wine-region bed and breakfast, an alpine retreat, a lake-side mansion, a grasslands hut, a cattle-station property. When it comes to rural property, the options are many — and the competition is huge.

To make money as a rural-holiday destination, wherever your property, it has to have an edge in such a crowded and diversified market.

Location is obviously still the main deciding factor, but it also helps if the property is within a three-hour drive of a major city, because it means your pool of potential tenants will be much larger. The Friday-night trek after a working week has to be within reason and many people aren't keen to travel anything more than three hours.

Also, many rural areas, like the coastal market, are also undergoing significant redevelopment. Old tennis courts, school halls and disused community grounds are being bought by developers planning to land-bank the properties until economic conditions are right. Whether you personally agree with this practice or not, what it signals is that a town or location has a bright future.

When you are planning to buy a rural property, keep an eye on local development and economic activity — such as development of new shops, expansion or renovation of existing shops, or establishment of a new industry or major employer. It may be a sign that the area is ripe for redevelopment and an economic upswing.

Tried and true

Check zoning on all rural property to see if it is in a bushfire-prone area. As well as alerting you to potential danger, it can also mean additional ongoing maintenance and signifies that fire retarding construction materials must be used.

Golf course property

It seems every time you look in the paper or turn on the television there is another high-profile golf celebrity launching a new golf course and housing estate. There are now hundreds of properties planned for this type of development around Australia.

Golf course property is proving a popular purchase; however, most of these properties are too new to give any indication of resale or income potential.

The attraction of a golf course home is similar to the lure of the sea for many people. The dream of being able to walk out the door and trundle across to the golf course for a hit is a big drawcard for many people. Adding to the attraction are the benefits of club facilities — such as social clubs, gymnasiums, pools and restaurants — that are often developed in conjunction with the estates and local councils.

How many ugly golf courses have you seen? By their very nature, golf course estates are usually in stunning locations surrounded by hectares of breathtaking rural or coastal scenery.

In some of the best-designed and well-planned golf course housing estates, you can feel as though you are one of only a select few in such a privileged location, despite your property often being one of several hundred homes.

Like other holiday-home markets, these properties are not necessarily bought to earn a permanent rental income — many people are buying them as potential retirement homes and renting them out in the meantime. Of course, other estates are being designed specifically for permanent residents, either tenants or owner-occupiers, like any other new housing estate.

Did you know?

Golf is one of Australia's most popular sports and has one of the highest participation rates of any sport or physical activity in the country.

Did you know? *(cont'd)*

There are 1.1 million people, or 7.5 per cent of the population, over 18 years old who play golf (890 000 men and 193 300 women).

Golf is fourth in popularity behind walking, aerobics and swimming.

Source: Australian Bureau of Statistics

Serviced apartments

Serviced apartments have always been a popular holiday-accommodation option, but they are now also available as an investment option.

Typically, serviced apartments are run by large hotel- or motel-style managers and are either owned by a parent company of the manager or by more traditional commercial-property investors.

Nowadays, they are often sold as individual units and bought by private investors, particularly residential investors.

Most major cities have had a surge in apartment development and most development will include a component of serviced apartments — in fact, some buildings will consist solely of serviced apartments.

An oversupply of residential apartments has been avoided by some developers, who choose to convert any unsold apartments in their developments into serviced apartments. These investors will often install a management company to run the complexes on their behalf, or to sell them to private investors, not as straight apartment purchases, but as serviced apartments with a ready income stream.

So, as well as assessing the property (location, scarcity value and construction), part of your purchase decision about a serviced apartment will include assessing the manager. In many cases you are simply buying an income stream when you purchase one of these assets; therefore, you need to be confident the manager is going to do a good job.

Some rental returns are guaranteed (such as those generated as a set percentage of annual yield), while some have a minimum guaranteed income and a top-up payment based on turnover or occupancy. Others can be solely based on occupancy levels. Therefore, the ability and experience of the manager to attract visitors is vital to your investment decision.

There are several income structures that can be used. At some developments, all the properties are put into a rental pool whereby each apartment has a designated rating, or points, in line with the value of that property. The owners are then allocated a share of the income on this basis, with some owners earning more than others, regardless of individual occupancy rates.

In other systems, however, owners get their income based on the actual occupancy rate of their apartment.

Serviced apartments are also being developed in coastal and regional areas as well as city locations. In some seaside and resort locations, the properties are often marketed to include a two-week 'owner's time' each year, as an added incentive to the rental guarantee or estimated income.

Questions you need to ask before buying a serviced apartment

As with other property investments, there are two ways to make money—from rental income and from capital gain. As part of the decision to buy into this type of property, you must ask yourself:

- What will the resale market be for this type of property?

- Who will want to buy it?

- What will happen when the management agreement runs out?

- What if the manager sets up a new development nearby?

....

Tax considerations

If you negatively gear a property in a holiday-home market, such as a coastal cottage or serviced apartment, you may need to get specialised tax advice if you also use it during the year for personal reasons.

The ATO allows investors to apportion part of their expenses against the period of time in which the property is available for rent; however, this can be open to scrutiny depending on what time of the year and how often the property was used for personal reasons.

If you use your holiday house during the peak period, such as summer holidays or the ski season, and only rent it out during off-peak times, when tenants are scarce, the ATO could rule that the property's primary purpose is as a personal holiday home and not as an investment. This could wipe out any chance of claiming a tax deduction for some of the expenses, such as interest costs, rates and insurance.

Even though you may have only used the property for four weeks (out of the 52 weeks in a year) you may not be able to claim expenses for the outstanding 48 weeks when you did not use it. In fact, the Tax Office could argue that you used it during the whole of the peak income-earning period (such as school holidays or summer) and, therefore, it could not allow any deductions.

For example, if you use a rural property every weekend and make it available during the weekdays, the ATO is also likely to frown upon a claim for five-sevenths of expenses, because, in reality, you are using it for 100 per cent of its major income-earning time.

This occurs because you are mixing personal use with investment use. As we said earlier in the chapter, it's a situation that rarely works and the two ambitions should be kept apart.

If you are not using your property for personal use, then holiday homes, serviced apartments, golf course properties, alpine retreats, and country cottages are like any other investment property — if the expenses outstrip the income, then the difference can usually be offset against your other income (in other words, negatively geared).

Financing

Just a quick note on borrowing money for a property in this market: the tourism or holiday markets can be fickle. Bad weather, political and economic change, and even fashion, can cause a major slump in some markets — and lenders know this.

Finding a mortgage to buy an investment property in a holiday market may take a bit of shopping around. Not all mainstream lenders are going to see it as such a great idea, because the list of risks and a history of low returns in that market will add to the problem. However, like most property loans, your ability to secure a loan will be judged on whether you can make the repayments and the bank's desired level of security.

While no-deposit and low-deposit property loans are available, it is unlikely that lenders will be jumping to lend on this basis for holiday-home purchases. Comments from recent holiday-home purchasers have indicated that some lenders require deposits of at least 20 per cent for some markets because of the sector's reputation for being uncertain.

Properties with income guarantees, such as managed golf course homes and serviced apartments, may make it easier to work out the returns to show the bank. However, the bank will also be making its own assessment on likely returns once that guarantee expires.

Chapter 13

Managing a
rental property

In this chapter we will cover the following:

▲ Tenants

▲ Determining the rent

▲ Management — agency versus do-it-yourself

▲ Landlord's insurance

▲ Bookkeeping ... back to the shoebox.

Buying a property can take a long time, especially if you refine your search and really hunt for a bargain. You will find yourself scrolling through websites and reading newspapers and agency booklets (and, of course, reading property books). Weekend after weekend will be spent at open for inspections, even before the auction or the negotiating process starts.

While eventually the property is bought and that part of the process is over, management of the property never ends. The good news is that the management of your property is far less intensive than searching for the right investment property to buy.

Managing a property always requires some work — at the very least, some decision making — and how much (or how little) is up to you.

There are many management styles, but some basic options are:

▲ You can get an agent to look after everything for you — meaning they will come back to you only when they need decisions made.

▲ You can hire an agent to find you a tenant and then you take over the rest of the ongoing management.

▲ You can run the whole thing yourself, from go to whoa.

Whichever way you choose to go, investment rental properties mean (hopefully) having tenants.

Good tenants pay on time. You may never hear from them, apart from a couple of years later when they move out, or when the inevitable maintenance or repair is needed, such as when the hot-water system fails.

Unfortunately, not all tenants fit into this category. Some are habitually a little late with the rent. Some are habitually very late with the rent. Some can be a little careless. And others simply don't respect the property they live in. All this can cost you money.

If a shiver just went down your spine, just remember that it's all part of property investment, and that you can usually insure against the worst of tenant damage.

For the most part, tenants are just normal people, but most property investors will have to deal with the odd problem tenant at some stage. Sometimes tenants just need a warning and they're back on track, while others need ongoing management.

Tenants

Once you have a property the next thing you'll need to acquire is a tenant — and not just any tenant. Finding and choosing tenants can spell the difference between a hassle-free investment property and one that is fraught with problems.

Even if you have an agent managing the property for you, if the tenants are a problem, the agent will still consult you on most management decisions and that can involve a lot of time on the phone and making decisions. Ultimately, it is your investment property — your risk, your reward, your responsibility.

The way to achieve the best return from your property is to attract long-term reliable tenants. The fewer tenancy changeovers you have, the better. Every time a tenant changes, you risk a period of vacancy plus you (or your agent) also have to conduct the whole screening and reference-checking process all over again. Spending a little extra time and taking a little extra effort finding the right tenants can pay off in the long run.

One way to reduce problems is to make sure your tenant is suitable for the property. For example, if you have a three-bedroom suburban house surrounded by families, then renting the property to a group of rowdy teenagers is bound to cause friction.

The last thing you want to deal with are constant complaints from neighbouring property owners and residents. There are legal remedies other tenants or property owners can pursue to stop nuisance tenants from disturbing their peace or enjoyment of their own homes — and these remedies might occasionally cause you some extra work.

If you have a one-bedroom property in an inner-city apartment block, allowing a tenant with two large dogs to rent the property could be asking for trouble in terms of property maintenance as well as the neighbours. Choosing the right tenant is an important part of ensuring your investment is a good one.

Determining the rent

When you establish the rental amount for your property, you need to ensure that what you are asking is achievable. The biggest factor in this decision will probably depend on the property cycle.

Ultimately, rents are set by the forces of supply and demand. If rental vacancies are low, you are in a landlord's market, when you, as the landlord, have the upper hand over tenants and will be more likely to be able to achieve the rent you want.

If rental vacancies are high, it is a tenant's market, when the tenant is in the strongest position. During periods of high vacancy, tenants may be able to ask for and receive discounted rent, depending on how long you — or your rival landlords — have been waiting for a tenant.

An internet search and a walk around rival properties for rent will soon let you know if the rent you are asking is reasonable. Also, keep in mind your target tenant when you are deciding on how much rent to charge. If your ideal tenant is a quiet, middle-aged person who will look after the property and take care of the garden, he or she may not be able to pay as much as a busy couple on two incomes who may not have as much spare time to devote to taking care of the garden.

Your aim, particularly in the early years of property ownership, should be to have the rent meet your outgoings (including the interest), or at least a sizeable portion of the total costs. The minimum rent, therefore, is easy to nominate — it's the maximum amount of rent that will take careful thought.

A lot of new landlords can be tempted to try for the maximum rent they can possibly achieve. By all means, give this a go if you want to, but it may mean several weeks or months of vacancy — with no-one helping you to pay the mortgage — and then you may still have to drop the rent.

How an extra $20 a week can affect the bottom line

A two-bedroom inner-city apartment is advertised for the estimated top dollar within its market of $275 per week. It takes an extra four weeks to find tenants willing to pay the higher-than-average rental.

The four weeks of vacancy have cost the landlord $1100 in lost income. Therefore, the total annual income over 48 weeks will be $13200.

If the property has an asking rent of $255 per week—the average for this type of property—and it had only one week of vacancy, the annual income across 51 weeks will be $13005.

The difference is small in the first year; however, the risk of losing the $275-per-week tenant will be high when the lease comes up for renewal, which may see you facing another four-week vacancy before finding another tenant willing to pay top dollar.

While you have $195 less income in the first year from the lower rent, the risk of losing the $255-per-week tenant is less—and because the price is the 'going rate' there is less reason for the tenant to move, which means a lease renewal rather than a vacancy. This also means no re-letting fee (usually one or two weeks' rent, $255 to $510) to be paid to the manager, no advertising fees ($150 or more), and no cleaning costs or other change-over complications and expenses—so you are rapidly ahead despite your initial lower rent.

Most managers and experienced property owners will tell you it is better to attract and keep a reliable tenant than it is to squeeze tenants for the maximum rent each time and risk them moving out when the lease is up for renewal.

As with buying and selling property, you need to play up the good points of your rental property to potential tenants. Whether you do this yourself or through an agent is your next big decision.

Management — agency versus do-it-yourself

Do-it-yourself (DIY) management will cost you less money and could be easier on your cash flow, but it might not necessarily be cheaper (depending on how you value your own time). A big part of the 'agency versus DIY' decision is how much time you are able to invest. If you don't have full-time employment or social or family commitments, you may decide to devote some of your spare time to managing your own investment property.

How much cheaper it will be depends on the value you place on your spare time to manage the asset. If you are 'time rich' and won't have to take time off work or away from family affairs, then DIY could be the best method. However, if you are 'time poor', the agent's management fee might be worthwhile.

Depending on the agency and the type of property, most people can expect to pay between 5.5 and 8 per cent of the rental income in management fees. There will also be other costs, such as letting fees and other special one-off fees for various services. This may sound like a lot, especially if your budget is restricted, but professional management does have its advantages.

Advantages of agencies

If you don't have the time or you don't want to be woken in the middle of the night to try to find a tradesperson to fix a leaking roof or a burst pipe, then professional management could be for you. Many agents have a 24-hour number for tenants to ring and, if it can't be put off until morning, the agent is required to tend to these things for you.

Agents should also be familiar with the numerous laws, regulations and protections governing landlords and tenants. If you DIY, you will have to learn these rules and ensure the administration and processes are followed or face potential legal action.

An agency will be able to ensure the lease is legal and executable. Managing tenants directly can be difficult and dealings must always be conducted within the rules of each state's tenancy laws. If a dispute does arise, a property manager will be able to represent you at any hearing at the rent tribunal.

A manager can also find and select a tenant. In many cases, agencies have many resources to draw on, including a register of previous tenants and professional screening techniques. A good manager should be able to resolve any disputes with a tenant before they get out of hand.

Handy hint

Most professional or experienced property investors use property managers. As well as saving time, it also removes any emotion from the relationship between tenant and landlord. As the owner of a property you may not be able to see the disadvantages of one property over another; you may not be able to negotiate with a tenant; or you may feel personally insulted if the tenant stops paying rent or causes you stress. Involving a third party in the management (an intermediary) can provide an independent buffer for both the tenant and the owner.

An agency usually has a range of professionals and tradespeople to call when something goes wrong with your property. It will be able to rely on these tradespeople for emergency and urgent repairs — something that can be invaluable when you have unhappy tenants or tenants who have little regard for safety. Agencies often also have agreements with those tradespeople, meaning that the tradespeople may give discounts to the agent's landlords if they get a lot of work from that agency.

However, while most agencies and managers say they can do all these things for you, the biggest challenge will be appointing one that really does follow through and make your life easier.

Bad agents can be awful to deal with. If you pay an agency to look after your property, but have to call every other month to ask why the rent hasn't been paid, why are you paying it?

Sales talk prompting you to sign a management agreement will undoubtedly include assurances that all your needs will be met and that you will be provided with a trouble-free investment that gives you a regular monthly income and no hassles; however, in reality, this is rarely the case. One of the most common complaints from property investors is about slack or bad management. This can arise because the tenant wasn't properly screened; a problem reported by the tenant was not responded to fast enough by the agent, making the tenant angry; or because the agent made decisions without even consulting the owner.

If you do choose to use a property manager — and most professional or experienced investors do — then you still need to 'manage the manager' and ensure he or she is giving you the service you want.

....

Handy hint

A few questions you might wish to ask when you choose a manager:

- How many properties do you have under management?
- What is your total vacancy rate?
- How long is your average vacancy?
- What is the reason for each current vacancy?
- How many full-time and part-time staff manage your properties?
- What is the ratio of properties for each senior staff member?

- How many years' experience do your staff (not directors) have?

- How do you screen tenants?

- What reference checks are involved?

- How will the rent be collected?

- What is the procedure when the rent does not arrive or is late?

- How do you deal with maintenance and repair issues?

- How often do you do a full inspection of the property?

- What is the procedure to find new tenants?

- What are the total and individual fees you charge?

- Under what circumstances would additional fees apply?

- How often and by what method do you make payments to the landlord?

- Can you provide the contact details of two existing landlords for references?

What each agent offers for his or her fee will vary considerably. Make sure you get in writing what services are included (or not included). Agencies will often have a pamphlet they give to prospective clients — keep a copy. Also make sure you have a letter detailing specifically what the agency will do for you and your property, including schedules of any regular meetings, commitments or 'to do' items.

Because agents offer a service, they add GST to their fees. Agents usually deduct the management fee and GST from the rental income, so that you don't have to physically write a cheque to pay your agent. Make sure the management agreement includes a provision that the agency must obtain your consent before deducting any money apart from regular management fees.

Advantages of doing it yourself

The most immediate advantage of DIY management is that you will not have to pay a management fee. As mentioned, this is usually around 5.5 to 8 per cent of the rental income (depending on the services offered), but it can be as high as 15 per cent for holiday homes. If you were to take 7.5 per cent (an average management fee) of an annual rental income of $15 600 ($300 per week) you would save $1170 a year.

However, against this saving you have to weigh up the time and expertise you will have to invest. Before making a decision it may pay to study your state's tenancy laws. These are usually available through your state government's website by searching under 'Residential Tenancy Act' or 'Residential Tenancy Tribunal'. Once you've spent a weekend reading the various legislations and processes, you may think twice about doing it yourself.

Besides the previously mentioned state tenancy laws, the sorts of things you need to become knowledgeable about, if you are considering DIY management, include local prices for rents and payment frequencies. On top of this, you must know how to:

▲ advertise for tenants

▲ prepare lease and bond requirements

▲ lodge bonds with trust accounts

▲ collect details and references from prospective tenants

▲ screen and check references of all applicants

▲ show prospective tenants the property

▲ arrange key and property handovers

▲ choose a tenant and execute a lease.

After this, of course, you will still have ongoing responsibility to ensure you meet the obligations of the tenancy agreement, make repairs, perform maintenance, review the rent and find replacement tenants.

At all times during this process, the tenant has the right to quiet enjoyment of the property. As the landlord, you must help ensure that this is the case. It means you can't go to the property or inspect whenever you want to — you will generally have to give fair notice that you intend to come to the property. In other words, for the term of the lease, it is the tenant's property — and you can't treat it as if it's yours.

Before you make your decision about DIY management, also ask yourself the questions listed earlier that you should ask a manager. Obviously the questions about staff numbers and experience will not apply to you, but you will need to have a plan for your property, which means being able to answer most of the other questions.

Landlord's insurance

We briefly discussed in chapter 8 the different types of insurance you should consider when you become a property investor. We'll now spend a little more time on the most important type of insurance when it comes to managing a rental property — landlord's insurance.

Landlord's insurance policies are specifically designed for residential investment properties. They include more detailed cover for the particular problems that can arise with an investment property, and are different from traditional building-and-contents insurance policies used to cover most properties.

Landlord's insurance policies may include cover for malicious damage by a tenant; accidental damage by a tenant; theft by a tenant; legal liability arising from tenants' actions; or protection against a tenant who does not pay the rent. Not all insurance companies offer this type of policy, and each company has slightly different clauses in its policies, so check out the premiums and fine print on exactly what is covered.

....

Handy hint

It is very important to have a thorough read of an insurance policy if you are doing the insurance yourself, or to quiz your insurance broker about why he or she is recommending this particular product.

....

Consider if something serious were to happen to your property, to the point where it becomes uninhabitable. As distinct from building-and-contents and liability insurance, landlord's insurance, which can often be taken out with the previously mentioned policies, is designed to cover loss of rent, or rent default and theft by a tenant.

If an incident that damaged the property were to occur — for example, a violent storm or negligent behaviour on the part of the tenant, such as a fire in the kitchen, whether accidental or not — you may be in for long periods in which the house cannot be rented. Landlord's insurance is designed to cover these instances. Check all policies closely, because they will sometimes cover you if a tenant breaks a lease early, stops paying rent or if the tenant is legally evicted from the building. Other things that you should check in the policy are the maximum the insurer will pay and any excess you might have to outlay.

Bookkeeping ... back to the shoebox

Good record keeping is vital for successful property investment. Property investment involves a lot of paperwork, much more so than other investment assets (like shares, for example).

As discussed in chapter 9, it's crucial to collect all your receipts in relation to your investment property. In the early stages of property investment, the thing you may well be most focused on is whether the rent arrives in your bank account or not — and rightfully so. But what happens if you only focus on the rent coming in and forget to ensure you claim all the important tax deductions? There are a lot of things that you may claim for the property during the course of a year. It will make it so much easier for both you and your accountant if you have everything in the one place when the end-of-year paperwork needs to be done.

That's why we suggest the shoebox method of bookkeeping. It's simple. It means you don't have to decide where in an alphabetised file you have to put a piece of paper. It means you don't have to leave it on the kitchen bench because you don't have time to work out where to file it. It means that everything can just be put in the shoebox and you know at the end of the financial year that it will all be there (not in the car glove box, not under the stack of phone books or accidentally wrapped up in the recycled newspapers). A shoebox may be low-tech but it works.

Chapter 14

When is it time to sell?

In this chapter we will cover the following:

▲ How long should you hold your property?

▲ Assessing the total returns to work out your sale price

▲ Opportunity cost

▲ Market cycles

▲ Preparing your property for sale

▲ Which selling method?

▲ Online marketing

▲ Beware of the conditioning process

▲ Capital gains tax.

How long should you hold your property?

This is one of the most difficult questions you will face with any investment. In some property circles the answer is forever. For these investors, the accumulation of wealth is based on buying and holding, not selling.

The decision about how long to hold your property is always hard, but it is particularly difficult with residential property. Property has the ability to provide a good return during the time you own it, from both rental income and capital gain, and it can be hard to justify selling. Even though you can't 'cash in' the capital gain until you physically sell, you can still borrow against it in the meantime, which is just as valuable, and provides you with more flexibility than cashing in your capital gain.

If you are paying off principal and interest on your residential investment loan, or your rent increases substantially over the years, you will eventually get to a break-even point — where your rent pays all the costs and interest on the property. In this situation, it is even more difficult to justify selling; the investment has basically become a 'set and forget' asset, which just ticks away quietly in the background with almost no input needed from you.

The same applies when an investment property provides positive returns, when the rent produces a profit after costs and interest. Rising rent usually keeps up with inflation (over the long term) and will provide a steady income to live off — so that apart from income tax, it's all yours!

At the same time, your property is also still clocking up capital gains as the value appreciates, which lets you borrow more against it to buy other property investments or diversify into equities or managed funds. In other words, it can sometimes be hard to justify a sale.

However, eventually many investors will sell, either to fund another area of their investment strategy, divide assets among family members or to fund a lifestyle change.

The 10-year guideline

Ideally, you should buy property with a medium to long-term investment timeframe in mind. This means a minimum of five years, but preferably 10 years. The rule of thumb for property is that the capital value should double within 10 years, although the capital gain will often double in under a decade. There are plenty of examples where the value has doubled in seven or eight years — depending on what part of the market cycle the property was purchased. However, if you stick to the rough 10-year guideline, it may help you in your decision about when to sell.

If you have held it for less than 10 years but have already doubled your money, then it may be a good time to sell. Depending on the phase of the market cycle, the next few years may see only modest price growth, so you may as well take your profit early.

If you are at the 10-year mark, or have passed it, and you haven't doubled your value, it may be time to cut your losses and find a property or area with better capital growth. However, properties that produce low price growth but high rental returns are still valuable assets, so factor the rental income into your decision-making process.

Depending on how you structured your purchase, and regardless of the increase in house price, it is the increase in equity that is your primary objective.

Assessing the total returns to work out your sale price

Okay, take out your calculator. Assessing your total returns requires a bit of paper shuffling and number crunching.

Before you work out your ideal sale price and sell, you need to know how much this investment property owes you — and it's not just the amount you paid plus interest. There are lots of other costs to throw into the mix before you can calculate a final sale price. Bear in mind, of course, that while you will still only get what the market is willing to pay, it does help to know how much you are owed.

It may seem complicated but it is still just a simple method for working out how much a property owes you. To have it calculated professionally, visit your accountant — who should also have your tax returns and depreciation schedule on hand to do a total cost and return analysis.

Table 14.1 shows the costs you will need to know to do your own calculations. You will also need them to calculate your cost base when you prepare to pay any CGT (see later in this chapter). So it's time to dig out that old paperwork.

Table 14.1: calculating how much a property owes you

Purchase costs	Holding costs	Selling costs
• buying price • taxes (stamp duty, mortgage registration) • legal and financial costs (conveyancing, lawyer, bank fees) • title costs (registration of title, land transfer fee) • building inspections • valuation fees • adjustments on purchase (such as rates and water adjustments).	• capital improvements /maintenance • interest costs • rates • water (and other services not covered by tenant) • insurances • management, administration, accountant fees.	• repairs/ presentation updates • sales commission • advertising • lawyer/ conveyancing • discharge mortgage/ bank fees • accountant fees • capital gains tax.

By adding all these costs together you'll have the total cost of the property. Now subtract from this the income you have received. If you have negatively geared the property, also subtract the tax savings you have made.

This revised amount will be what the property owes you. In most cases it will be a lot less than your expected sale price; however, it is necessary to know this figure inside out in case you are pressured on auction day to accept a lower price because there is only one bidder.

Opportunity cost

If you want to be really hard-nosed about this investment, you could also include the 'opportunity cost' or, in some cases, the 'opportunity lost' of owning this particular investment. It is a brutally honest method of judging an investment that takes into account what you could have done with your equity had you not bought the property in the first place. The following example shows how you would calculate the opportunity cost for a five-year property investment.

Example—a typical five-year investment:

$35 000 property deposit (equity not borrowed)

$15 000 for fees (equity not borrowed)

$7000 for repairs, rates or insurance (equity not borrowed)

$14 000 for the net interest cost (after rent received)

$71 000 in total costs (equity)

To work out the opportunity cost, you have to decide what you could have done with the $71 000 during the same five-year holding period. You need to ask yourself questions such as:

- If you had made deposits into an online savings account, earning 5 to 6 per cent a year over the

Example *(cont'd)*

past five years, how much would the deposits have grown to?

- If you had gradually purchased company shares or units in a trust, during the five years, with the $71 000, how much would you have grown the investment to?

....

This exercise also works as a comparison of investment types, and while it is not a necessary process for working out the sale price for your property, it is still an interesting exercise to do when you are thinking of selling.

If the property has not produced a great rental return compared with a savings account, then the location or building type hasn't compensated you enough for the risk you took, especially compared with a no-risk investment such as a bank savings account.

If managed funds have grown well beyond what you could ever have hoped to get from your investment property, perhaps the location or building type wasn't such a good choice and you may need to rethink the value of this investment.

The outcome of this exercise may help you decide if you should sell or not and, if you do decide to sell, how much you could expect to receive to justify buying property as compared with other types of investments.

Market cycles

Property markets run in cycles of roughly 10 to 12 years. By timing your sale (and purchase) you can take advantage of this recurring phenomenon.

Undersupply

At the beginning of each cycle there is strong demand from buyers and renters for property and generally not enough property for everyone — this is the 'under supply' phase of the cycle. During a period of undersupply, property prices go up strongly because there is more competition from people wanting to either buy or rent. People often outbid each other to offer a higher purchase price or higher rental just to secure the property.

If you are selling during this time it is known as a 'seller's market'. If you are renting out a property during this part of the cycle it is known as a 'landlord's market'. In other words, the seller and the landlord get to call the shots.

During an undersupply phase, developers quickly swing into action and start building. They see that the prices being achieved for existing properties are rising and the returns are usually well above the construction cost to build new properties, which means there are profits to be made.

Even supply

As the number of properties increases and the demand from buyers and renters is gradually satisfied, the market goes into the even-supply phase — where the number of houses and the demand from people wanting to buy or rent is roughly equal.

Keep in mind that this is not an exact even supply. In a rental market, for example, there is usually about a 3 per cent oversupply (or vacancy rate) because it allows for the usual movement of tenants between properties.

During an even-supply phase, prices are usually either fairly steady or experience only small rises. There is no great urgency from buyers at auctions or sales to help push prices higher and tenants usually have a choice of a few properties, so rents stay pretty even too.

Oversupply

Eventually — and it seems to occur no matter how many lessons or cycles we go through — the market hits 'oversupply'.

During an oversupply phase, property prices and rents can fall. You do not want to be a seller during this time. It is known as a 'buyer's market', or a 'renter's market', because the buyer and the renter call the shots.

In the oversupply phase, the developers have built the new properties and satisfied the demand from buyers and tenants, but instead of stopping, they keep building. The reason this happens is because the buyers and the tenants have got a taste for the new properties and, since they have the choice, are switching out of the older, established homes and into the new ones.

It's a bit like moving house to follow fashion or a trend! The newer properties usually have added benefits — such as more technology, an up-to-date design or modern fittings — that give them an edge over some of the existing property.

So as the developers keep building and the buyers and the tenants keep buying and renting, an oversupply — often of older property — begins where no-one is interested either in buying or renting. This is the over-supply phase of the cycle.

The best way to insulate yourself against the negative effects of an oversupplied market is to own a property in a good location and one that is in high demand no matter what phase the market is in.

Each phase of the cycle lasts about three to four years, so if worse comes to worst, you will probably only have to sit out three years of oversupply before regaining any lost ground — which is somet to keep in mind if you are trying to decide when to sell.

Preparing your property for sale

If 'location, location, location' is the first rule of buying property, then 'presentation, presentation, presentation' is the first rule of selling it. To get the best price for your property, you need to make as many people as possible want to buy it. You can't change the location or the building type but you can make sure the presentation is the best it can be.

Presentation does not mean renovating or redecorating, it means making the most of what you have and highlighting the good points. You should also aim to eliminate any bad aspects or anything that will make someone stop and think twice about buying your property.

Unless you are selling a renovator's delight, buyers do not want to pay for things they have to fix. So fix that broken window, tile, sticking door, broken light fitting and wonky letterbox. Don't expect someone to overlook it, just because you've been overlooking it in the past.

The first impression is always the most important. That means making sure the front of the house or apartment building is looking its best. Street appeal is a major drawcard. It also acts as a very strong pre- and post-purchase reinforcer — a marketing term that means people want to have their decision reinforced. Nobody wants his or her friends or family to drive by the property he or she intends to buy, or have just bought, and for the friends to think that it looks shabby or bad. Everybody wants to buy a house that 'looks' like it's a good buy!

If there is a front garden, make sure it is weeded, neat and tidy. The same goes for the fence and the front door — give it a wash, or even a lick of paint, to give a good first impression.

If the property is in a block of flats, clear or tidy any junk mail in the public area; make sure the rubbish bins are stacked in the designated area; and let fellow occupants know you are selling and that you'd like to give a good impression.

The key areas for top-notch presentation inside your property are the kitchen and the bathroom.

Kitchens

The kitchen has two major functions. The first is that it has to be workable. It has to be a place where people can efficiently prepare, cook and store food. That means buyers will be assessing cupboard and bench space, as well as any built-in appliances. If you can maximise your bench space — even by making it just appear larger — you'll go a long way to satisfying many buyer's needs.

The second major function is harder to define. It's an emotional function. A kitchen is often referred to as the 'heart' of a home, which conjures up the image of family and friends gathering together to share their day as they prepare a meal. For this, bench space or the number of cupboards is irrelevant. What you need to do to meet the emotional need will vary with each buyer, but generally it means creating an inviting space — somewhere people can imagine working, confiding, taking time out or entertaining. It is easier to define what is not inviting than to pinpoint what is. A dark, windowless kitchen, for example, is uninviting. A tacked-on wooden addition at the back of the house is also unlikely to appeal to many people. Likewise, benchtops covered in mess and clutter, an enclosed room or a room shut off from the rest of the house, is also unwelcoming.

Cleanliness is the ultimate aim for a kitchen. Even if it is a dark, galley kitchen added on to the back of the house, if you ensure that it is clean and provide stools, a chair or small table so that the person cooking doesn't have to be alone, then you are halfway there!

Bathrooms

The bathroom is another room that usually must fulfill the two functions of being practical and emotional.

While the practical aspects of a bathroom are obvious, by adding a few special presentation touches you can also appeal to the emotions of a buyer who may be looking for a luxurious escape from everyday stress.

First tackle the practical presentation issues. Mould — get rid of any sign of it. Broken or chipped enamelware — replace it or touch it up. If the bathroom is dirty or missing tile grout — replace it or touch it up. Cleanliness, once again, is your main aim.

Now for a few extras. Extra-thick towels, candles, scent and even a fluffy white bathrobe draped over a chair can all help give an impression of indulgence, even in the tiniest bathroom.

Throughout the property

Overall, while the house should look clean and tidy, one of the biggest demands from people these days is for more space. High-density living has made extra space a premium that many people are prepared to pay for.

If possible, make areas within the house more versatile. If you have an area under the stairs, for example, set it up as a study with a computer desk. If there is a bay window in the lounge room, you could set up a lounge chair and side table to make it an enticing reading area. Also, a small table in the kitchen can double as a quiet place to have a cup of coffee and read the morning paper or as extra workspace; an old bench seat nestled under an arch in the garden suddenly opens up the option of a garden retreat; or by setting up an outdoor table and chairs in the car-parking area, you will be emphasising the versatility of a small off-street parking spot.

Another way to create a feeling of space is to take furniture away. You may be accustomed to the way a property looks, but it's possible every room can do with the removal of at least one piece of furniture, if not two.

As a final experiment, when the property is ready for sale, ask a friend or family member to take a slow walk through the inside of the property and around the outside and take notes of what someone might consider 'discount' material — something a buyer will stop and think twice about. It could be a muddy path to the front door, curtains that don't hang properly or a screeching doorbell.

Small details can make a difference and usually cost next to nothing to eliminate. But remember that this exercise is no good if you do it yourself. Human nature being what it is, you will probably disregard things you don't think are important and not write them down on the list. However, it's not about you — it's about your buyer. By getting a third party to perform the task it is much more likely that you will eliminate any discount points.

Tenants

In many cases, you will be selling your investment property complete with tenants. This requires delicate diplomacy, especially if you would like to improve the presentation.

Speak honestly with your tenants, tell them what your plans are and why you are selling the property — they could be potential buyers!

You will need to follow strict legal requirements when arranging open for inspections and conducting the sale itself. Each state has tenancy rules and regulations, which you can check yourself on the website of your consumer affairs or fair trading office. Also speak to the managing agent, who should know these regulations by heart, and see what he or she can suggest to ensure everything runs smoothly.

In some cases, it may be worth selling the property without tenants. This may mean hiring furniture and homewares to present it well.

Bear in mind that regulations can require giving tenants several months' notice of your intention to sell. Potential investors may prefer that a tenant is already in place, because it means that the property is earning income from the day the new buyer takes over.

Which selling method?

The selling methods for property in Australia are private sales and auctions.

Private sale

Most properties across Australia are sold by private sale (private treaty), despite all the attention given to auctions. However, there are still several ways to treat a private sale and a discussion with your agent, and your local knowledge, should make it easier to decide which method is best in your case.

The main issue to consider with a private sale is how to price the property.

Price setting

You have several options for letting potential buyers know what price you are looking for. They include:

▲ fixed price — you state the price you want (most buyers will offer under this)

▲ price range — you offer a price range, with your ideal price somewhere at the top of the range

▲ price plus — this usually involves stating your lowest figure and asking for more, such as $350 000 plus

▲ tender — you don't give any official price or range but ask people to nominate a price in a tender (the details remain confidential)

▲ expression of interest — similar to a tender in that you ask people to nominate their price (again, the details remain confidential).

Sole agent or multiple agents

You can choose to either list the property with one agent or you can list it with two or more agents. Multi-agent listings could mean that none of them will really work too hard because an agent may be pipped at the post by rival agents, despite several weeks of hard work. On the other hand, sole-agency agreements mean you can list your property with one agent and only that agent has the responsibility for selling it.

Auctions

Auctions are popular for properties that traditionally have high demand and a large number of potential buyers. The ideal auction is one that has several bidders competing with each other and wildly bidding! In reality, this rarely happens.

Inner-city properties, high-profile properties, unique properties, or any property in a very tightly held market, are often auctioned. The reason these properties work well at auction is because they compel anyone interested in buying the property to come to the sale on that day and at that time. The fear of missing out on a rare, sought-after, hard-to-find or one-of-a-kind property is usually enough to ensure the buyers will turn up.

If the property is run-of-the-mill, then there is no gripping reason for buyers to turn up on the day — especially when a similar home will be just around the corner.

However, in an undersupply phase of a market cycle, other properties can also sell well at auction. This is because there is usually more demand to buy than there are properties for sale, which will create competition for your property and potentially push up the price.

The location of the auction can also influence potential buyers. If the potential buyer is standing in front of the house or in the garden of the property, then there is a stronger emotional pull to make sure he or she 'wins'. If the auction is in the rooms of an agent or other location, where all there is to see and feel is a projected photograph up on a screen, then there may be less emotional pull.

Online marketing

Including your property on an agent's individual website and also through a specialised national and international real estate site will help you get the greatest potential exposure.

Most real estate agencies use online marketing to ensure they get the widest and easiest exposure for their clients. Online marketing enables people to 'shop from home' and can take a lot of the leg-work out of buying a property.

Ideally you would like your property to receive as many 'hits' (people looking at your property on a website) as possible from potential buyers, so you will need to discuss this with your agent to make sure the agent's website will cross-reference your property by using as many search parameters as possible. Your property can be located or 'hit' based on several factors, including:

▲ price range

▲ location

▲ number of bedrooms

▲ size of land

▲ proximity to schools.

Beware of the conditioning process

All most people want to hear from an agent is that their property is going to be easy to sell and will get more money than they had hoped for. However, often it is not quite as simple as that, leaving the seller (and buyer) on a slippery slope.

Some real estate agents use a tactic known as 'overquoting'. They will overquote or inflate the estimated sale price to the seller in the hope they will secure the job to sell the property. In turn, they often 'underquote' to potential buyers to raise their hopes about what they can afford to buy, and to, perhaps, push buyers a few extra thousand dollars higher.

During the marketing period, both the seller and the buyer undergo the conditioning process. The seller is gradually told that 'the demand just isn't there' at the initial (inflated or overquoted) price, while the buyers are told that 'the demand is much stronger' than the initial (deflated or underquoted) price.

Then comes the 'crunch'. The best time for an agent to crunch the deal is at an auction when emotions are high and the buyer and the seller are being asked to make on-the-spot decisions. This also applies to private sales, when both the seller's and the buyer's hopes have been raised, and they are both asked to compromise.

This is another reason why you should know your bottom line when it comes time to sell — or at least be aware of the conditioning process and be prepared for it. By working out how much a property owes you well before the sale process gets underway, you will be in a stronger position to make your final decision on the price you will accept.

Capital gains tax

Capital gains tax will have a big impact on the final profit from the sale of your investment property. CGT is a tax on the profits from the sale of investments, including property investments. Changes to CGT laws over the years have produced a multi-tiered tax regime. How much CGT you pay now depends on when you bought your investment. As always, make sure your accountant or tax adviser is involved in helping you determine your CGT issues.

You purchased a property before 20 September 1985

If you purchased your investment before 20 September 1985, then you do not have to pay CGT on the profit. In other words, you have a tax-free investment — congratulations! While the capital gain is tax free, you will undoubtedly have paid tax on the income from the investment over the years.

You purchased a property after 20 September 1985 and before 21 September 1999

Any investment property purchased on or after 20 September 1985 will attract CGT. But there are different rules for properties bought between 20 September 1985 and 20 September 1999, and for those bought on or after 21 September 1999.

To estimate how much tax you will have to pay, you need to establish your cost base. The cost base is the purchase cost and all the other related costs you haven't been able to claim as a tax deduction during the period you have held your investment.

The extras you can add to the cost base include stamp duty, legal fees, titles office fees, selling fees and the agent's commission on sale. Basically, they include any buying, holding or selling costs that have not been claimed against income.

These costs are added to the purchase price to establish the cost base of the property. The amounts are adjusted in line with inflation up to 30 September 1999 (when indexation ceased), based on when the expenses occurred, and the profit is established after the inflation-adjusted figures are deducted. You will also need to include any amounts you have claimed as building depreciation over the years as this too will have an impact on the final figure. The CGT is based on your profit, and it is levied at the rate of your personal marginal income tax rate.

Deciding between the inflation-adjusted and 50 per cent discount rules

If you purchased your property between 20 September 1985 and 20 September 1999 you have an additional CGT option. You can either assess the CGT based on the inflation-adjusted method described above, or you can choose to work it out using the 50 per cent discount rule that was introduced from 21 September 1999. This gives you the option of choosing the method that produces the lowest CGT liability. However, the inflation-adjusted method becomes less useful with every year past the end of the indexation period in 1999.

From 21 September 1999

If you purchased your property on or after 20 September 1999, as long as you have owned the investment property for more than 12 months, CGT is calculated using the 50 per cent discount rule. After you have established the cost base and know your final profit or capital gain figure, the difference, or profit, is then reduced by 50 per cent and that figure is taxed at your marginal income tax rate.

Your tax adviser or accountant will be able to assess your exact CGT position. Tax tables and indexation tables are also available on the ATO website.

It's important to remember that you only pay CGT when you sell. If you don't sell, you don't pay — which is another reason to think carefully about your decision on when to, or if to, sell.

Chapter 15

Alternative property assets

In this chapter we will cover the following:

▲ Property trends

▲ Buying an income stream

▲ Buying for capital gain

▲ Hidden potential

▲ Assessing the tenant and the lease

▲ Shops

▲ Industrial property

▲ Offices

▲ Specialised funding.

Property trends

Years of rising residential real estate prices followed by uncertain future capital growth have encouraged investors to look elsewhere in the real estate market — and commercial property has been a logical alternative. Because it traditionally carries more risk than residential real estate, commercial property offers the potential for higher returns, substantially longer lease terms and lower ongoing costs.

During the past five years, particularly in the last couple of years, first-time investors have flocked to commercial property across Australia. Compared with residential rental returns of as little as 3 per cent, commercial assets offer rental returns of up to 10 per cent — and often that is after most of the holding expenses have been paid by the tenant, which is known as a net return.

Most first-time commercial investors begin by tackling an investment that is relatively small and work their way up from there. In the majority of cases, this is usually a local shop or small office. Like residential real estate, these assets are often within a short distance of the investor's home or in a familiar area.

Self-employed businesspeople also often invest in a commercial property and lease it back to their business. This used to be the most common way to be a first-time commercial property investor and includes all kinds of businesses from panel beaters and builders to doctors' rooms and accountants' offices.

However, rather than looking at buying something to use as your own business premises — which can include decisions outside typical investment rules, such as guaranteeing the business can keep its location — our book looks at buying commercial property as a straight real estate investment. A search through <realcommercial.com.au> will give you an insight into the variety of commercial properties available for sale.

Traditional residential investors have been making waves in the commercial markets for a few years now. Demand for property from first-time commercial investors has been so strong that it has been attributed to a surge in prices, particularly in retail property such as local shops and small supermarkets.

Typically, commercial investors are more focused on rental returns — the longer term capital gains are often secondary considerations. While some commercial property investors do buy for capital gain reasons, in most cases, particularly with purpose-built factories or warehouses, the investor aims to make the majority of profits — if not the whole return — from income alone.

Buying an income stream

The tenant pays the outgoings for most commercial property leases. Outgoings include council rates, body corporate fees, insurances and some maintenance. So, as the owner, the money you receive each month is usually the net return, after most of the costs associated with owning and renting a building have been paid. Of course, interest costs on any borrowings, as well as land tax, are your responsibility and are not included in the tenant's outgoings.

Unlike residential property leases, commercial property leases cover significantly longer periods. Often, the shortest commercial lease will be three years but they can also be as long as 10 or 15 years. In comparison, most residential leases are for periods of 12 months. Therefore, buying commercial property is often likened to buying a long-term income stream.

In the commercial property world, everything is quoted as a net return or net yield. Real estate agents, investors, managers and vendors all talk about the income after the outgoings have been paid by the tenant.

Rents are also quoted on an annual basis, not weekly or monthly (as with residential property).

Commercial properties are advertised to tenants on a net basis, and at an annual rate that has two components to it. The first component is the net annual rent, which is based on a rate per square metre. The second component is the total annual outgoings, which is also often quoted as a rate per square metre, but it varies depending on what bills come in during the tenancy.

For example, an office may have a sign advertising the property for lease at $300 net a square metre. If the office is 100 square metres in size then the annual rent will be $30 000 a year (100 × $300 per square metre). Most lease agreements divide this up so that it can be paid monthly or quarterly.

On top of the $30 000 net annual rent, the tenant will also pay the outgoings. For a small office the outgoings could be another $4000 a year. This could be quoted as the net annual rent plus outgoings of $40 per square metre or as an estimated lump sum of $4000. The tenancy agreement will spell out the finer details of these outgoings, but they usually cover all bills associated with the property during the lease period.

In comparison, residential property investors have to pay the outgoings and holding costs from the gross rents they receive from their tenants.

Generally, when you are searching for a commercial property to buy, it will be advertised as offering, say, $50 000 net rent. (The outgoings are rarely mentioned because these are shuffled off for the tenant to pay.)

From this net rent of $50 000, you need to think backwards to work out what yield or return you want. With $50 000 net rent, for example, if you want an 8 per cent annual return, your offer price has to be about $625 000. Likewise, if you are willing to accept a 7 per cent return, your offer might be $700 000, and so on.

At a commercial property auction you will be bidding against someone else who has his or her own limit based on a desired annual return. The higher the price you pay, the lower your annual return as a percentage.

Buying for capital gain

Despite the focus on generating an income stream from commercial property, there are also genuine capital gains to be made from the commercial property markets.

Retail property (such as shops, shopping centres, show rooms, restaurants and supermarkets) has probably shown the strongest capital gains in the past five years, as first-time investors and seasoned investors have flocked to these popular, small commercial assets.

Unlike most commercial-property assets, shops are probably the exception to the rule of buying for a high income stream. In many cases investors are prepared to buy on annual returns (yields) as low as 3 or 4 per cent, without any expectations of earning higher rent in the short to medium term. The historical increase in capital gains from this sector has been enough to keep luring investors — despite the low rental yields — because they believe they will make a profit when it comes time to sell.

There is usually little or no capital gain from many commercial properties. This can be the case with factories or warehouses, which can be virtually obsolete by the time the tenancy expires (although the land may still retain some value). However, most commercial investors will try to earn as much as possible from their rent, rather than relying on making a profit from capital gains when they sell.

Unlike residential property, commercial property also runs in a cycle that is linked more closely to the economic conditions of the time. This is because business and commerce is affected much more by the economy — and, therefore, commercial property fortunes — than individuals, wage earners and residential rental property are.

Different states and even different suburbs have varying economic conditions. A high-profile retail precinct is less likely to feel the downward pressure from a cut in consumer spending than a poorly patronised or badly located shopping centre in the same town.

Commercial property cycles are also quite predictable and roughly run on a 10- to 12-year cycle: undersupply, even supply and oversupply.

During the oversupply phase there is no new development and prices of existing commercial buildings fall. This remains the case until business demand picks up again and it turns to undersupply, then even supply, and then the cycle starts over again.

The phases of the cycle have a big impact on capital gains and rents. If you have to sell your property or find a new tenant during a period of undersupply, then the chances are you will do well and make a capital gain or earn a higher rent. If, however, you have to sell or find a tenant during an oversupply phase, you may be disappointed with the offer price and be forced to drop the rent.

Of course, on the plus side, you may get a bargain entry point by buying during an oversupply period. Remember that for every transaction there is a buyer and a seller — and both have competing ambitions.

Hidden potential

An ability to see hidden potential will often be the difference between a mediocre investment and a fantastic investment. For example, buying an old service station with only a few years left on its lease might look on the surface to be a risky purchase. As an investor, you are unlikely to earn anywhere near a good return during the last few remaining years of a lease; however, it may still be worth buying it for other reasons.

Service stations are usually in reasonably developed and sought-after locations, surrounded by residential or small commercial precincts. The future uses of an old service-station site are many, such as housing, offices or shops. The type of neighbourhood — the location — will dictate the potential of the property once the lease expires. However, always talk to the local council about rezoning or decontaminating such a property before you factor this potential into your purchase decision.

If you think there is an ongoing use or a new use for a property, then it is worth considering as part of your purchase assessment. Even if you do not want to necessarily become a developer and build a new apartment project or a small office building on the site, the property may still be a good buy.

Instead of just sitting and waiting for the lease on the old service station to expire, you could be doing the groundwork by getting permits and rezoning in place so that you're ready for an instant resale to a new buyer once the lease ends. Developers sometimes pay a premium for properties that already have permits and plans approved.

Another example may be a shop with just one year left on the lease. While you will carry the risk of losing the tenant after a year and having to find a new one — possibly with a period of vacancy in between — by taking a closer look at the lease you could find hidden potential.

If the rent has fallen below the market rate for that particular shopping strip, and the lease restricts future increases, then it could be well worth buying the asset on a low yield, such as just 4 per cent. You could then factor in a higher rent and more frequent or market-based rent increases, once a new lease is written. This will boost your annual return to a higher percentage.

A word of warning

Leases may not always be as they seem. Just as some leases include amounts under market rates, there are also some that feature inflated rents—which may not be sustainable in the long term.

Assessing the tenant and the lease

Just like with residential property, if there is an existing tenancy, it is vital that you assess the tenant and the lease before you purchase commercial property.

The lease

It pays to seek expert advice and guidance when it comes time to assess a lease for a commercial property. If you have narrowed down your search and are serious about the potential property, it is wise to consult a commercial lawyer and ask for an assessment of the lease. At the very least it will ensure that your expectations are met, and at most it will stop you from making a terrible mistake and perhaps being locked into a long-term deal that you can't afford.

Commercial real estate agents can help with this. Remember, they are not lawyers and if you want to reduce your risk on a property, have the lease thoroughly scrutinised by a commercial property lawyer. After all, in a commercial property deal, the lease is actually more important than the bricks and mortar.

The terms of a lease put a legal obligation on you and your tenant. Both parties need to fully understand what the obligations are.

In your case, as an investor, the lease governs every aspect of that all-important income stream. The terms and conditions and clauses of the lease will cover subjects such as:

▲ rent increases (how much and how often)

▲ use of the property (type of business that can be operated there)

▲ guarantees (who you can turn to if the rent is not paid)

▲ outgoings (how much and what bills the tenant will pay)

▲ collapses (what happens when things go bad, when there are disputes, or when there is a need for debt recovery).

One of the hidden dangers in buying a commercial property is an artificial rent. This means the rent is artificially high and not sustainable. Make sure the rent stated in the lease is realistic — a commercial valuer should be able to assess this for you — so that you don't get caught when the first term expires and new tenants refuse to pay as much.

If it is a short-term lease or you are planning to redevelop or install your own tenant, then the sitting tenant will need to be given the appropriate notice. How this is done and how smoothly it happens will also depend on the terms written into the lease. The lease should detail what happens when the lease expires, how much notice must be given and what condition the property must be left in.

Most commercial leases have a 'make good' clause that requires the tenant to remove anything he or she has added, and to restore the property to the same physical condition as when the tenant moved in.

The tenant

Just like the residential property market, the tenants of commercial properties are not always perfect.

If you strike a troublesome tenant, you need to be aware of the often lengthy and costly procedures that need to be followed to have the situation resolved — 'lawyers, guns and money' is the typical saying when a lease comes into dispute. What this translates to is a lot of time, bad feeling and money.

When problems involve somebody's livelihood, such as your tenant's business and your income stream, the stakes can be extremely high. That is why it is also a good idea to make your own personal assessment of a tenant.

Questions you should ask yourself when assessing tenants

- Do you think the tenant is running a successful business?

- How experienced is he or she at this type of business?

- What history does the tenant have with the property?

- What guarantees (bank or personal) does he or she offer?

- What is the tenant's reputation in business and the community?

You will have to make these assessments yourself, and local knowledge and talking directly to the tenant will help you make up your mind. Rival real estate agents — not the ones trying to sell the property or trying to lease it — can also be a very good source of information, as can other tenants and owners of nearby properties.

What every investor really wants is a 'blue-chip' tenant. These are usually large multinational or national organisations, such as the big supermarket chains and well-known corporations.

A blue-chip tenant is like a blue-chip share or investment — it's the one that is the least likely to fail.

However, these tenants are almost exclusively found in the domain of major commercial shopping centres and huge office buildings, and are unlikely to be found in the local shops or neighbourhood commercial project. But the theory behind their rating can be extended to any tenant. The most important issue is whether the tenant will be able to pay the rent each time it's due and whether he or she will be able to stay in business for the full term of the lease.

Shops

Shops are the most popular investment for first-time commercial-property buyers. Shops have a lure that no other commercial property seems to offer. The attraction appears to have its roots in people's familiarity with the type of business and location of most shops.

Whether it's the local milk bar that is for sale, a small fashion shop in a high-profile retail strip in your suburb, or perhaps a city-fringe all-night café — most first-time commercial investors usually go for retail property that they know.

Most commercial agents say that first-time purchases usually cost less than $1 million and are often around the $500 000 mark. At this price range, retail real estate is easily comparable to residential property.

Retail property is probably the lowest-yielding commercial asset; however, it still offers high returns compared with residential property.

Retail property in prime suburban retail strips probably offers the lowest incomes within the retail sector. For example, in the current environment, a small shop in a high-profile retail strip would typically offer a yield of about 5.5 or 6 per cent a year, while a shop in a less desirable outer suburb could return closer to 8 per cent. However, the long-term difference between the two is the future potential capital gain.

The prime suburban retail strip will have a history and a potential future of much higher capital gains than the single cluster of shops in the outer suburbs of the less-desirable location.

That means the investor buying the shop with a 6 per cent return is banking on getting a bigger capital gain to top up the lower returns from the rent. So, the total return is the rent plus the profit on reselling the property.

The investor who buys the less well-located shop — the shop with an 8 per cent yield — is expecting to earn more of the total return from the rent, with less profit to come from the eventual capital gain when the property is resold.

However, the property with the 8 per cent return is also a risk because it is in a less-desirable location. A property in a less-appealing location may not attract a tenant when the existing lease expires, or a buyer when it's time to sell.

Industrial property

Industrial property is often the overlooked 'ugly duckling' of the commercial property markets; however, it can make an excellent investment.

Factories, warehouses, workshops and manufacturing plants are very unglamorous but are among the highest-yielding commercial assets in Australia. Returns from small industrial properties are often 10 per cent net or more. The catch is that they can also have the lowest secondary demand, from future tenants and future buyers.

Nowadays, many factories are purpose built to suit particular tenants. This means that the building size and specifications are designed specifically for the first tenant. Once this tenant leaves, it can be tough finding a replacement who wants this particular building design or location. Although this is not always the case, it is an attitude that persists among industrial property investors. Therefore, these investors become used to earning the biggest part of their returns from rental income — hence the relatively high yields of 10 per cent or more.

However, buying a small factory or warehouse unit with a long-term tenant can be a profitable and low-maintenance investment and there is always potential for some capital gain or redevelopment.

Drive around your nearest industrial estate and look at the types of property there. Usually they will include a mix of industrial buildings, such as old saw-tooth roof factories, big stand-alone warehouses, clusters of contemporary industrial 'units', and a few combined office and warehouse (or factory) buildings.

These locations have advantages and disadvantages. Industrial estates are popular with developers and investors because a variety of industries and tenants can usually operate in them without any planning or local-government restrictions. The purpose of industrial estates is to keep similar loud or dirty industries contained within the one suburb or district.

On the downside, the future use of an industrial site and building will be restricted to an industrial use. It is unlikely that there will be a higher or better use for a property in an established industrial estate — which means you will be locked into an industrial market.

Take a drive through the residential areas near industrial estates and look at the older industrial properties that are often mixed in with the houses and the shops. You'll find the occasional workshop, panel beater, furniture factory or warehouse. These small industrial properties may seem like eyesores in an otherwise good area, but they often have great potential.

Old industrial properties in changing locations usually have future potential beyond what they are being used for today. The panel beater, for example, that is flanked either side by a milk bar and a residential house could be redeveloped as either a shop or a house, or maintained as an increasingly rare site with a permit for industrial use.

As our metropolitan populations expand, so too do the future development options for these older industrial buildings. You do not necessarily have to undertake this redevelopment yourself, but anything that offers an edge when it comes time to resell or find a new tenant will add to the property's value — and your returns.

Offices

Take a look at any city skyline and you will see towering office buildings of all shapes and sizes — lights and signs ablaze. These glamour assets of the commercial property market make headlines in property circles. Office buildings either make or break an investor's fortune.

The value of office towers goes up and down with the economy and business confidence. If confidence is high and the economy is up, businesses employ more people to fill up office buildings, which means more rent for the investor. However, when confidence is low and the economy turns down, so too does employment. Redundancies and corporate mergers mean fewer staff and, therefore, less demand for space to rent, which equals less income for the landlord.

Like any commercial property, the value of office buildings is in the income stream (rent). It doesn't matter how many architects designed it or how much granite was used in the foyer, if there are no tenants, it's almost worthless.

Smaller suburban office buildings are the same—no tenant means no value. Yet unlike their big-city cousins, small suburban office buildings don't have multimillion-dollar price tags. Often they can be bought for just a few hundred thousand dollars.

Suburban office buildings offer yields somewhere between the shops and factories; shops being relatively low for commercial property and factories being at the higher end.

At the time of writing, in most markets, suburban office buildings should deliver a net return of between 7.5 and 9 per cent a year. These figures indicate a pretty sound investment for this sector, because it means less risk in terms of location and tenancy.

A lot of office development in the last 10 years has been 'unit style'—where clusters of small office units have been built and leased as individual units to single tenants. These small units can also have doorways knocked through between adjoining units to cope with requirements of bigger tenants.

This type of complex often draws a wide range of tenants, from self-employed accountants, to call centres, medical practices and technical workshops. To an investor, this means plenty of potential tenants and future buyers. The wider the pool of tenants and buyers the more chance you have of earning a higher rent or making a capital gain.

Strata title offices are also growing in popularity with investors, developers—who are building and on-selling them—and owner-occupiers.

Entry-level prices for some strata offices can be as low as $200 000, with potential returns of about 7 per cent. For many residential investors, purchasing a strata title office is often their first move into the commercial market, probably following only shops in popularity.

Strata offices are typically smaller than office units or stand-alone suburban office buildings. However, like a strata title apartment or a residential property, strata offices should have their body corporate rules and regulations checked before you sign on the dotted line. In some strata office projects, the property is also locked into service-supply contracts, such as contracts with electricity or telephone companies, which need to be carefully scrutinised.

Specialised funding

Most finance lenders require a larger deposit — possibly up to 40 per cent — from you when buying commercial property. Interest rates for commercial property loans are also traditionally higher than those for residential real estate loans, because of the higher risks.

Finance lenders believe that there is generally a higher chance of obtaining a tenant (albeit at a discount) for a residential property — even if it means the investor has to move in. In contrast, there may not always be a business wanting to lease a commercial property (even at a discount) — and the investor certainly can't move in!

Although lease terms are significantly longer for commercial property than they are for residential property, vacancies can also be significantly longer. The risk of lending for commercial property is not only linked to the investor's ability to make mortgage payments, but it is also related to the tenant's ability to pay the rent.

Commercial property lenders will scrutinise the lease and the tenant before lending any money. They will try to assess the risk of the tenant going bust and what recourse they will have if it happens. Overall, the lender will be focusing on how to lower its risk, and, if all goes wrong, how to get its money back or sell the property. Some lease terms will affect the lender's ability to sell a property under forced conditions.

Lenders, and their valuers, will take into account the annual yield of a commercial property and also the purchase price paid based on the number of square metres of building area.

Most commercial properties have an estimated price based on the size and type of the building. For an office building the price-per-square metre may be $2000 for a particular market, while a shop may have a price of about $3000 per square metre for its particular market.

As well as looking at the yield, a valuer will also look to see if the purchase price is roughly within the market range for the type of property it is. If it is extraordinarily high, there is more risk the investor has paid too much. If it is too low, then it could be a bargain and indicate a lower risk for the lender.

Chapter 16

International property

In this chapter we will cover the following:

▲ The world property market

▲ Popular locations

▲ Added twists — politics and distance

▲ Foreign currency exchange rates

▲ Interest rates

▲ International red tape.

The world property market

We can't finish this book without a word on international property. A lot of people dream about a country home in the south of France, a garden bungalow in Bali or a deserted seaside shack on New Zealand's rugged South Island.

International property is no longer just the domain of the rich and famous. It is in reach of many property investors. International property is also a good way to diversify your investment portfolio because it means you are getting exposure to a different economy and property cycle.

The search and selection of overseas property is certainly easier than it ever has been. In many cases, the country and the region will already be known to the investor. Not only are Australians very well travelled, but we are also a nation of immigrants — Europe, Asia and the Pacific are traditional, ancestral homes for many Australian families.

That means we have an added reason to look overseas for investment property. Sometimes family members are still in those countries and they can help with the property selection and ongoing management. They should, at the very least, be able to help cut through the red tape to ensure your purchase and settlement go smoothly.

Like many Australian holiday and investment homes, overseas properties can easily start out as investments and eventually become a main home or an exclusive holiday home. Choosing an investment property in a country to which you might be planning to relocate will give you a foothold in that market ahead of your arrival, as well as enable you to earn income in the meantime.

Even without relatives in the chosen country, buying overseas property is not only a way to diversify your portfolio, it is also a good reason to travel each year to inspect your investment (which will also be partially tax deductible) and in many cases, investors can choose to spend a significant part of each year living at the property, while renting it out to holiday-makers from different countries at other times.

Depending on the local economy, arrangements can also be made for staff to be on call for the tenants and available all year round to keep up basic maintenance and management.

One barrier that you may find difficult to overcome without a bit of local networking is language. Be it French, German or Indonesian, it is unlikely that your school-learned language skills are going to be enough to see you through. If you don't have local contacts you trust, you will have to pay for expert advice.

Popular locations

Internet searches make narrowing your property search a cinch. By doing your groundwork through the internet, you can cut your time and expenses drastically. Not only are you able to do virtual tours of properties, but you can also browse cities and towns on various mapping and geographical websites.

Furthermore, you can search government websites for regulations and the foreign investment guidelines of the country you are considering, to help cut time and money when trying to meet the red-tape requirements. A lot of foreign government websites now have an English-language option you can click on.

Most countries have rules about foreign ownership of property. Check these out first before you start looking at property. In some countries the regulations are fairly relaxed. However, increasingly, they are being tightened and require some commitment to the country, such as a period of residency, a business or an investment venture.

New Zealand

One of our closest neighbours, New Zealand, is a popular country in which to buy international property. Unlike Australia, it does not have stamp duty on purchases, nor does it have land tax or

CGT. So when it comes to buying, holding and selling, your chances of making a profit are higher because your costs and taxes are lower.

In some situations, the ATO may also allow you to deduct any interest costs associated with your New Zealand property against your Australian income. In other words, you may be able to negatively gear your New Zealand asset against your Australian income — but check with your tax adviser first.

New Zealand's five largest banks are actually owned by Australian institutions, so much of the lending criteria is similar.

However, New Zealand has recently tightened its foreign ownership laws, after concern that prime beachfront and heritage-area properties were being snapped up by overseas buyers.

Special permission is usually needed for overseas buyers if they want to:

▲ spend more than $NZ50 million buying land anywhere in New Zealand

▲ buy land of more than 5 hectares on an offshore island

▲ spend more than $NZ10 million buying on an offshore island

▲ buy land of more than 0.4 hectares if it adjoins a historic or culturally sensitive area such as a lake or reserve

▲ buy land of more than 0.2 hectares adjoining a foreshore.

There may be other occasions when foreign investment approval is required; however, the application process is fairly straightforward. Decisions are usually made within a month through the Overseas Investment Office, which is part of Land Information New Zealand.

Did you know?

In November 2005, a United States man became one of the first people to be convicted of breaching New Zealand's overseas investment property rules.

He was fined $NZ17 000 for failing to meet conditions of foreign ownership over a 43-hectare property he purchased in the South Island town of Queenstown.

As part of the purchase, the man was given approval on the grounds he developed an orchard and tree plantation on the property that would create three jobs.

Three years later he had taken no steps toward these developments, other than to start foundation work for his holiday home.

Source: Land Information New Zealand

For more information on buying property in New Zealand, contact the Real Estate Institute of New Zealand <www. reinz.org.nz> or Land Information New Zealand <www.linz. govt.nz>.

Europe

In the 1950s, many European families migrated to Australia. They came from countries including the United Kingdom, Italy, Poland and Greece. Australia has received immigrants from almost every European country you can think of—giving a lot of Australians a strong connection back to Europe and a reason to consider buying property there.

But even those people without a European connection have probably heard reports of investors picking up cheap villas in the Greek Islands or stone cottages in Ireland, not to mention the growing number of investment opportunities in former Soviet countries.

United Kingdom

Unlike a lot of countries around the world, Britain does not have foreign ownership restrictions for Australians who want to buy property. But that doesn't mean it's all plain sailing — there are, of course, local customs you should get to know.

The best and easiest way to do this is to make friends with a local real estate agent — which you can do easily by email. As with any property deal, it is up to the buyer to beware. However, most agents in Britain act as buyers', as well as sellers', advocates, so they are able to let you know the downside of deals if you hire them to find you a property.

The biggest difference between buying Australian property and UK property is the time factor. Things seem to take a lot longer in the UK. It can be several months from the time you make an offer on a property until the time it is accepted and finalised. And even then there is the possibility of being 'gazumped' — a term used to describe someone overbidding an already accepted bid — right up until the transferral of ownership.

Most buyers also hire a structural engineer or surveyor to inspect and report on the property before they make an offer, or they make the offer subject to the findings of the report.

Fast fact

Investment property is known as 'buy-to-let' in Britain.

When you buy a property in the UK the costs can include:

- ▲ conveyancing fees (about 1 per cent of purchase price)
- ▲ search and disbursement fees (up to 200 pounds sterling)
- ▲ land registry fee (based on purchase price)

▲ stamp duty (based on purchase price — although some postcodes are exempt)

▲ survey costs

▲ mortgage fees.

Just a word of warning, flood problems (estimated to affect about one million homes) in the UK have meant some insurers won't offer insurance cover, or will do so, but only at a huge cost, so check with the local authority about inland flood-prone areas.

For more information on buying UK property see the UK trade and investment page at <www.britaus.net>

France

Perhaps drawn to this region by its relaxed lifestyle, Australians are rapidly joining the throngs of Europeans buying their slice of French provincial life.

Here are a few tips about buying in France. You will need to do your own homework before taking the plunge. It is especially important to get legal advice before you sign a contract in France, as most contracts will stipulate that you forfeit your deposit if you do not go ahead with the purchase.

There are basically two ways to kick-start the purchase of a house in France, either through a contract, such as a 'Compromis de Vente', which binds both the vendor and the buyer from the day it is signed, or a 'Promesse de Vente' which basically allows a three-month period when the vendor will not sell to anyone else. In both cases the purchaser will likely have to forfeit the deposit if he or she doesn't go ahead.

Buying a house on a small piece of land, usually one hectare or less, is fairly straightforward and requires minimal government approvals. However, buying farmland or a vineyard or other larger land areas will require special permission.

Unlike most countries, where each party has its own lawyers working on the transaction, in France you usually have the one official — known as a 'notaire' — who acts for both parties and follows the laws of the country to complete the sale and ensure everything is done correctly.

The notaire is independent (a bit like a bureaucrat) and will not usually be able to give you specific advice. So if you need to structure the purchase in a particular way or hit a snag, the notaire's assistance might be limited and you will need to get your own legal opinion.

This is particularly so with French death or inheritance laws. If, through your will, you intend to leave your French property to people of your choosing, then you need to get expert advice before signing any form of contract. This is to ensure the purchase is made in a way that will avoid the property being caught up in France's succession laws. If you are taking a mortgage against the property, this also must be noted at the time, along with the details included in the initial purchase contract.

Greece

There are about 2500 Greek islands sitting in the sparkling seas around Greece. They are just waiting to be enjoyed — each of them has valuable real estate. Buying property on a Greek island or the mainland is one way to ensure your place in the sun. However, purchasing property in Greece involves various taxes and fees that potentially add about 15 to 20 per cent to the purchase price. There is also usually a hefty property-transfer tax of about 11 per cent plus various other costs such as a notary, and lawyers' and registration fees. Deposits on real estate purchases are often higher than other markets, often up to 30 per cent.

If you are intending to rent out your Greek property you might also need a licence from the Greek Government, particularly if it is a tourism-style venture, such as a property rented to international holiday-makers.

For Greek and European Union citizens there are few restrictions — although sensitive border and coastal areas may be excluded or require special permission for purchase — but you will need to get government approval for most real estate purchases.

It pays to have a local English-speaking lawyer. The lawyer will be responsible for registering the purchase with the Greek authorities, ensuring all taxes are paid and that documents for the transaction are completed and lodged properly.

You will also have to nominate a public notary. All real estate contracts must be validated and signatures witnessed by this notary. The notary is responsible for registering the documents and ensuring the transfer goes ahead according to the legal requirements. As the buyer, you will also need a Greek tax number, which must be quoted on most documents. It can be applied for through the Greek Government.

For more information on purchasing property in Greece, contact the Greek Government through its website, <www.mfa.gr>. There is an English language option to click on if needed.

Bali

Many Australians think of Bali when they think of Asia, and the Indonesian island offers great property potential — even though it is unconventional compared with traditional Australian property ownership.

House prices in Bali are a fraction of what most Australians would expect to pay for the locations. They are also a fraction of the prices paid for holiday homes in high-profile Australian beach towns and are often in breathtakingly beautiful settings.

However, you will need to be cautious about titles and legal issues in Indonesia. In most cases, the only way a non-Indonesian can make a claim to any property is through a long-term lease, 'Hak

Pakai', of about 25 years. This is not a freehold title and in most cases can't be secured against a mortgage.

You may also need to prove you have an investment or contribute in some way to the local economy before you can take an interest in Bali property.

Your first step in any property search should be the Indonesian Government's website or a phone call to an English-speaking property lawyer who can help discuss the options.

In some situations you may be able to buy a long-term lease through an overseas investment company or unit trust. You may also be able to use a local nominee owner. As attractive as Bali and Indonesia are to Australian property investors, you will need to carefully scrutinise any agreement and have all documents checked by local and Australian lawyers to make sure all the facts are known and local regulations are understood.

Tried and true

For any overseas purchase, consult a property lawyer in the country in which you are considering a purchase before you start thinking about signing a contract.

Often, local real estate agents recommend someone; however, this may not be in your best interest—even though it is tempting to accept a ready-made referral.

It is better to consult someone totally independent. It will give you peace of mind, potentially save you from being misled and will avoid jeopardising your relationship with the agent.

Added twists — politics and distance

Buying an international property is similar to buying a property in Australia. The key purchase decisions are basically the same, but with a few added twists.

To start with, you need to narrow down your location (which country, which region and which district) and then decide the physical type of property you want to buy. A browse on website <realestate.com.au>, with its wide range of international links, will help you in your search of most countries (for UK property, <propertyfinder.com> is useful, and for New Zealand property, <allrealestate.co.nz> is also good resource).

Add to that the type of tenant you hope to attract and the amount of income you hope to earn. Those four factors will assist you in your purchase decision, the same as if you were buying in Australia.

When you are buying international property you there are a few extra considerations that include:

▲ Politics — is there a stable environment, one not subject to constant change, which can mean changes to foreign investment laws?

▲ Economy — how strong is the local economy, both the country as a whole and your region in particular?

▲ Tax laws — how will they affect your investment returns? Check with the ATO to see if there is a double-tax arrangement with the country involved.

▲ Housekeeping — how will you oversee the management of the property?

▲ Finance — how will you arrange your finance? How will you bring back profits?

Foreign currency exchange rates

At some stage when you are buying an international property you will have to factor in exchange rate differences between currencies. In the world of high finance, this is known as 'currency exposure'.

To help avoid some of the ups and downs of a currency exposure, you should consider obtaining a loan in the country where you are purchasing the property. As property income and mortgages will all be based on the same currency, and the same economy, it will make it easier to keep track of how your investment is going. That way, it is only when you bring your profit into Australia — or have to top up the overseas account — that you need to consider the exchange rate difference.

Most overseas banks allow internet access to their websites which means you can log on and track rental deposits and deductions on a regular basis, as well as make electronic transfers when you need to.

Alternatively, you can help reduce some of the risk of having currency exposure from an international investment by buying a 'hedge' or insurance product. Hedges and similar products reduce your risk by effectively smoothing out the ups and downs of currency. For a fee, many institutions will let you set a maximum or minimum range within which the currency may fluctuate. If it goes outside this range your hedge kicks in and you will not suffer the extra exposure. Seek advice from a financial expert (like a bank, stockbroker or a financial planner) for specific details if you are interested in how these products can help you.

Interest rates

Interest rates are also often quite different between countries and there may be significant points of difference between Australian interest rates and those of the country you choose. This may also factor into your decision about having an Australian-based mortgage or one in the country in which you are buying. In bigger, more stable economies, the chance of interest rate movements is usually more predictable. In smaller and more volatile economies, interest rates can swing without warning.

International red tape

There is no getting around it — buying international property can involve a lot of red tape. Each country has its own set of laws and its own special regulatory hurdles to overcome. However, you can do a lot of the work yourself without incurring the cost of high-priced experts.

Much of the groundwork for purchasing a property can be researched over the internet or through local embassies of the country you are considering. Most countries have a department that specialises in foreign investment, and countries generally welcome foreign investment in one form or another.

However, property investment can be a sticking point, because the ownership of land is a politically and culturally sensitive subject for many countries. That is why real estate usually has its own set of rules on foreign ownership that can be more strict than the rules concerning other types of investment.

....

Handy hint

Things you should check before buying an overseas property include:

- Are foreigners allowed to buy land in the country?

- What are the limits and restrictions on foreign ownership?

- If foreigners aren't allowed to buy land, what other form of title or ownership is available?

- Which government department approves foreign purchases?

- Email or write to this department and obtain its advice (straight from the horse's mouth, so to speak).

- If possible, narrow down the region or the area you are considering buying in — some countries have even more

Handy hint *(cont'd)*

> restrictions if an area is particularly sensitive, while less significant areas may have more relaxed rules.

- What taxes apply to property?

- What taxes do foreign owners pay?

- Does Australia have a tax treaty with this country? In some cases you can avoid paying double tax (tax in both countries).

- What private costs or agency costs or commissions are involved?

- What building restrictions or planning rules apply to properties?

- Check with the local regional government about development rules.

- Find out what legislation controls renting out the property.

- What types of insurance are required?

Once you are armed with the basic information about the country you're looking at buying property in, you can start seeking specific advice from a lawyer or government agency to proceed with the purchase. This basic preparation could cut hours and hundreds of dollars from the cost of buying overseas — not to mention reducing the stress of trying to deal with an issue you have no knowledge about.

Appendix: renting versus buying

Year	Rent	Rent running total	Accumulated difference (rent v interest)	Accumulated ahead (renter v buyer)	Mortgage	Mortgage interest	Interest accumulated	Mortgage principal accumulated
1	$14040	$14040	$9665	Renter	$28921	$23705	$23705	$5217
2	$14461	$28501	$18531	Renter	$28921	$23328	$47032	$10811
3	$14895	$43396	$26560	Renter	$28921	$22924	$69956	$16809
4	$15341	$58737	$33708	Renter	$28921	$22489	$92445	$23241
5	$15802	$74539	$39931	Renter	$28921	$22025	$114470	$30137
6	$16726	$91265	$44731	Renter	$28921	$21527	$135996	$37553
7	$16764	$108029	$48959	Renter	$28921	$20992	$156988	$45463
8	$17267	$125296	$52110	Renter	$28921	$20418	$177406	$53965
9	$17785	$143081	$54128	Renter	$28921	$19803	$197209	$63084
10	$18319	$161400	$55134	Renter	$28921	$19145	$216354	$72861
11	$18869	$180269	$54532	Renter	$28921	$18437	$234791	$83344
12	$19435	$199704	$52767	Renter	$28921	$17680	$252471	$94586
13	$20018	$219722	$49616	Renter	$28921	$16867	$269338	$106640
14	$20618	$240340	$44994	Renter	$28921	$15996	$285334	$119556
15	$21237	$261577	$38818	Renter	$28921	$15061	$300395	$133426
16	$21874	$283451	$31004	Renter	$28921	$14060	$314455	$148288
17	$21530	$305981	$21459	Renter	$28921	$12985	$327440	$164225
18	$23206	$329187	$10085	Renter	$28921	$11832	$339272	$181313
19	$23902	$353089	$3219	Buyer	$28921	$10598	$349870	$199637

Appendix (cont'd): renting versus buying

Year	Rent	Rent running total	Accumulated difference (rent v interest)	Accumulated ahead (renter v buyer)	Mortgage	Mortgage interest	Interest accumulated	Mortgage principal accumulated
20	$24 619	$377 708	$18 565	Buyer	$28 921	$9 273	$359 143	$219 286
21	$25 358	$403 066	$36 070	Buyer	$28 921	$7 853	$366 996	$240 355
22	$26 119	$429 185	$55 860	Buyer	$28 921	$6 329	$373 325	$262 947
23	$26 902	$456 087	$78 066	Buyer	$28 921	$4 696	$378 021	$287 172
24	$27 709	$483 796	$102 830	Buyer	$28 921	$2 945	$380 966	$313 148
25	$28 540	$512 336	$130 302	Buyer	$28 921	$1 068	$382 034	$341 000
26	$29 397	$541 733	$159 699	Buyer	$0	$0	$382 034	$341 000
27	$30 279	$572 012	$189 978	Buyer	$0	$0	$382 034	$341 000
28	$31 187	$603 199	$221 165	Buyer	$0	$0	$382 034	$341 000
29	$32 123	$635 322	$253 288	Buyer	$0	$0	$382 034	$341 000
30	$33 086	$668 408	$286 374	Buyer	$0	$0	$382 034	$341 000
31	$34 079	$702 487	$320 453	Buyer	$0	$0	$382 034	$341 000
32	$35 101	$737 588	$355 554	Buyer	$0	$0	$382 034	$341 000
33	$36 154	$773 742	$391 708	Buyer	$0	$0	$382 034	$341 000
34	$37 239	$810 981	$428 947	Buyer	$0	$0	$382 034	$341 000
35	$38 356	$849 337	$467 303	Buyer	$0	$0	$382 034	$341 000
36	$39 507	$888 844	$506 810	Buyer	$0	$0	$382 034	$341 000
37	$40 692	$929 536	$547 502	Buyer	$0	$0	$382 034	$341 000
38	$41 913	$971 449	$589 415	Buyer	$0	$0	$382 034	$341 000
39	$43 170	$1 014 619	$632 585	Buyer	$0	$0	$382 034	$341 000
40	$44 465	$1 059 084	$677 050	Buyer	$0	$0	$382 034	$341 000

Index

Acknowledgements

Bruce Brammall:

First, I would like to thank Genevieve, my beautiful wife, who has put up with an extended period of her husband being otherwise occupied for almost anything else while bunkered in his study. I thank her for her patience. Had it not been for all her ironing, lonely shopping trips and taking over of responsibility for almost everything in the kitchen, at least two major projects now wouldn't have reached deadline. My stomach, in particular, thanks her. I hope our recent trip partly made up for my poor availability as a husband.

I also want to thank Gen for her journalistic skills — even after I'd worked over something 10 times, she was still able to suggest dozens of improvements. She can also spot stupidity (generally) and unclear writing (specifically) from a different room. There were many concepts to simplify. She has probably saved me plenty of embarrassment.

Thanks go to my co-author, Karina Barrymore. Thanks for bringing me on board. I think we made a good team.

To Allison Purdey, thanks for your valuable legal advice. I know that a bottle of wine (even a nice one) is considerably less than your going rate, so I hope you also received a warm inner glow from helping out a friend.

My appreciation also goes to *Herald Sun* photographer Andrew Tauber for the back-cover photograph.

To my family (Mum, Dad and Dirk), I hope you know that I appreciate the great examples you've always been to me.

Karina Barrymore:

Thank you Steve and Molly. You are my only true home.